A HISTORY

A HISTORY

THE
DONNING COMPANY
PUBLISHERS

Dedicated to the memory of
Lucy Levy
who did more for Achille's reputation
than he did.

Barbara A. Bolton, Project Director

    The Donning Company/Publishers
    184 Business Park Drive, Suite 106
    Virginia Beach, Virginia 23462

Library of Congress Cataloging-in-Publication Data

A. Levy, A History/by Bank of A. Levy
   p. cm.
  Includes index.
  ISBN 0-89865-638-9
  1. Bank of A. Levy—History. 2. Levy family. 3. Ventura County (Calif.)—Social conditions. I. Bank of A. Levy.
HG2613.V44L4814 1991
332.1′23′0979492—dc19

Printed in the United States of America

Contents

Introduction

The history of Bank of A. Levy, surprising though it may be, begins in a small French village called Mommenheim. There, on October 23, 1853, Abraham Levy was born. During his childhood, Abraham was nicknamed "Achille" by his family. He would be known by this name for the rest of his life.

Joseph and Francoise, Achille's parents, made considerable sacrifices to send him to a private school in Strasbourg. He did exceptionally well there in "compabilité commerciale," translated as business aptitude. Not much is known about his childhood. Joseph died when his children were young, leaving the family in need of money. For this reason, Achille left school at the age of 15 and found employment at a drapery store in Strasbourg. He worked at this business for the next three years, until 1871. During this period, the textile trade was a most promising vocation for a young Alsatian. Achille's future was bright; however, the world political scene would soon give his future an unexpected turn.

Prussia, led by Foreign Minister Otto Von Bismarck, completed its campaign against France in September of 1871. The French flag, flown over Strasbourg since 1648, was taken down and replaced by the crowned eagle of Prussia. For the next half century, Alsace was part of the German empire.

Several weeks after the German occupation, a concentrated effort was begun to mold the Alsatians into German citizens. The French language was suppressed by means of a decree which pronounced that no school could use or teach it. Meetings, both in public and private, were conducted only in German. French theaters were closed to French plays. French

1

signs over shops were changed to German. The name of the province was changed from Alsace-Lorraine to the Germanic Elsass-Lothringen. To use the French phrase "à bientôt" (the future looks good) became treasonable. Bookshops were forbidden to sell any of the works of standard French authors. Those who were discovered to belong to the underground Alsatian nationalist "League of Patriots" were fined and imprisoned.

The German secret police was very active and invaded both private homes and businesses. Strasbourg became a military garrison, with thousands of German troops housed in public buildings and private homes. Young men had to register in the local military headquarters or be considered deserters from the army. Restrictions were placed on business practices and commercial establishments were forced to give favored status to German products and consumers. Alsace became a subordinate colony of the German empire. Its inhabitants enjoyed few rights.

Within a few months of France's defeat, Achille Levy wrote his employer a letter of resignation. It was written in both French and German, so as to comply with the censorship laws.

Achille did not simply leave Strasbourg, or even Alsace, but France itself. In 1871, he made his way to the United States. He was not alone. By the end of 1872, over 270,000 Alsatians had officially changed their nationality and left Alsace. He was one of an estimated 600,000 Alsatians, fully a third of the pre-war population, who left their homeland over the next three decades. Most of these emigrants relocated in France, but a significant number continued across the sea and did not stop until they reached the coast of California.

In late 1871, Achille arrived in San Francisco, with the help of financial aid provided by his uncle, Isidore Weill. Weill operated a store in Dixon, a small town close to San Francisco. Achille's business education was very helpful to him there. Through his work experience in the store, he learned conversational English.

Achille remained in his uncle's employ for about two years. During this time, he became acquainted with a Mr. and Mrs. Wolff. In 1873, at their behest, Achille left Dixon for Hueneme. There he worked for their son, Moise, who was the owner of the town's general merchandise store. In Hueneme, Achille began his new life, eventually becoming partners with Wolff and forming what would be the first of many successful business ventures.

Chapter I

The Land of Opportunity

When Achille moved south to Hueneme in 1873, the process of splitting up Santa Barbara County into two parts was almost complete. Ventura was established as an independent county that year. Though Hueneme was a small village with limited conveniences, it had its own wharf, from which local produce was loaded onto freight vessels. Being the only deep water port between Los Angeles and San Francisco, it served as the center for agricultural operations of southern Ventura County. The wharf had been engineered and built by Thomas R. Bard, who would later be the only Ventura County citizen elected to the U.S. Senate.

The Hueneme Pier

In September of 1875, shortly before his 22nd birthday, Achille was honored by being appointed

U.S. Postmaster for the town of Hueneme, even though he was not yet a citizen. Because Hueneme was considered a "transient" village, the post office was in Wolff's store, as was common practice.

Achille became a U.S. citizen on November 6, 1876. In this same year, he became a partner in Wolff's store, a store soon to become known as WOLFF & LEVY. The two partners hit it off together personally as well as professionally, residing in the same house on Market Street for nearly five years.

Achille's business ventures were well planned and reflected an astute appraisal of Ventura County mercantile needs. As their 1877 invoices and stationery promised, Wolff and Levy provided everything one might want, and then some:

> "Highest Market Price Paid for Country Produce.
> Dry Goods, Clothing, Boots and Shoes, Hats,
> Hardware, Crockery, Groceries, Paints, Oils, Yankee
> Notions, Fancy Goods, etc.
> Agents For All Kinds of Agricultural Implements."[1]

Toward the end of 1881, after enjoying nearly six years of commercial success, and the accumulation of friends and customers throughout Ventura County, Achille looked forward to something more personally fulfilling; the establishment of a new business, and the creation of a family.

Achille had planned a store in Springville as early as 1881, evidenced by his having acquired new stationery with the heading of "A. Levy and Co., Springville."[2] Springville, which no longer exists, was a small trading community located between the present sites of Central Avenue, Wood Road, and Highway 101, southwest of present-day Camarillo. While the exact date for its founding is unknown, the store was in existence from 1881-1885. Moise Wolff oversaw the operations while Levy was in Europe in late 1881.

Levy, in need of money for his trip to Europe, invited Moise to be his partner in the Springville enterprise. This explains why stationery and invoices exist with "A. Levy & Co., Springville," blocked out and stamped over with "Wolff & Levy, Hueneme." At the top of the invoices, the order of the names of the partners was reversed and is listed as "Levy and Wolff." It has been suggested, in the past, that Wolff and Levy dissolved their partnership before Achille left for Europe and that this was how Levy obtained the money for his trip. This seems unlikely. The official dissolution of Wolff and Levy is on record as having occurred March 1, 1885, four years after the initial founding of A. Levy & Co., Springville.

In pursuit of a wife, Achille left for Europe in the latter part of 1881. With $50,000 earned from the sale of half of his interest in the Springville store, Levy embarked on a comfortable voyage to France. He had sufficient funds to engage the services of a marriage broker, or *shadchan*, then customary among the European Jewish community. In addition, he had the security of an income from the ongoing firm of Wolff and Levy to look forward to upon his return.

French village

After visiting his mother and sister in German occupied Alsace, Achille returned to Paris. The marriage
broker had found Lucy Meinette Levy, Achille's 42nd
cousin. This Parisian socialite became a charming companion and helpmate to Achille for the next 40 years.

Achille and Lucy Levy's daughter, Julia

The details were quickly accomplished, and on
January 8, 1882, Mademoiselle Lucy Levy was married
to Monsieur Achille Levy de San Francisco. Achille
may be excused for the affectation, as few Parisians
had ever heard of Hueneme. They had a very short
honeymoon, and Lucy and Achille left Paris within a
month. The journey back to Hueneme was not a plea-
sure cruise, as Lucy was soon forced into service as a
nurse to Achille, who was seasick during much of the
voyage to New York.

Levy marriage certificate

After a cross-country railroad trip to Los Angeles, Lucy confronted a new challenge. Upon their arrival in Ventura County, Achille and Lucy faced the steep descent of the Conejo Grade, later known as the Lewis Grade, the only way from the Conejo to the Oxnard Plains. Recent rains had made the trail so slippery that the stage hands had to chain the front wheels to the coach to the back wheels to prevent it from overtaking the horses. The stage driver requested all passengers, including Lucy, wearing her Parisian finery, to walk down the trail. Taking gown in hand, she made the two-hour descent. The trail was steep and muddy, but Lucy took this in stride, describing her entrance to the Oxnard Plains as a "novelty."

9

Stagecoach

Lucy's frontier spirit tempered her surprise at the small size of Achille's Hueneme house. The three rooms contained no plumbing, hot water nor bath tub. She termed the Hueneme house "surely interesting." Whatever doubts Achille may have felt about the ability of this refined woman to adjust to the primitive life of this rural American farming community were soon laid to rest. The Levys modified and enlarged the little house, creating beautiful flower gardens to satisfy their mutual, life-long fascination with roses. A tall wooden fence on the west side of the home stopped the predictable afternoon breeze from damaging their roses. A front porch offered Achille a place to enjoy his beloved cigars, the source of some friction between the newlyweds.

Achille's homecoming meant a somewhat reluctant return to the firm of Wolff and Levy. While he continued to enjoy the steady income from his old business, plans for a business of his own had pre-

The Levy's first Hueneme home

occupied him even before his trip to France. Achille began an independent agricultural commodity brokerage firm in Hueneme soon after Lucy and he set up residence there. In addition to this new business, Achille was still engaged in the joint partnership with Moise Wolff, which lasted until March of 1885.

The last public notice of Wolff and Levy on record is mentioned by E. G. Gerberding, the editor of the local newspaper, the *Ventura Democrat,* on February 12, 1885. He suspected that the firm of Wolff and Levy, a bastion of the business community, was on the way to dissolution.

As is the case with any partnership dissolution, it is difficult to know all of the reasons that led to their decision. There had been disagreements over management style, and the fact that these men both worked and lived together contributed to their difficulties. The private house system, the practice of boarding the clerks of one's business establishment, worked well initially; however, by the time Lucy returned with Achille, and Anna Levy was born, there were seven people living together. The place was overcrowded,

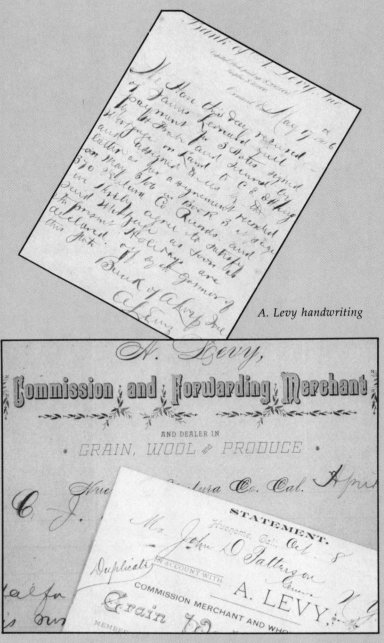

A. Levy handwriting

A. Levy bank draft

and relations between the owners of Wolff and Levy became strained. There were rumors of a fist fight between the two on a public street.

The two men dissolved their joint ownership of the residence on Main Street on August 1, 1884. They began proceedings to terminate and divide their assets, including both private and public holdings. On December 3, 1884, Wolff and Levy sold, for $550, what was potentially the most valuable piece of real estate in their possession. Block G, in the City of Hueneme, was situated on the north side of Broad Street and comprised over two hundred feet of frontage. Moise and Achille had entertained high hopes for the future when they purchased the lot in 1873.

Between December of 1884 and March 1, 1885, the date determined for the final dissolution, much advice was offered to each of the partners as to their final decision. Lazarus Weill, an uncle of Achille who owned a mercantile store in San Luis Obispo and who also had legal training, was concerned about Achille's lack of experience in the legal aspects of the dissolution of Wolff and Levy. Achille had written him early in February of 1885 concerning the matter and included a copy of the dissolution agreement. Correspondence between Achille and his uncle appears to have strengthened his resolve to strike out on his own. On March 7, 1885, Moise made his final offer to sell the firm to Achille, who refused. During the ten days that followed, $150,000 was settled on as the total worth of the Wolff and Levy partnership. On March 17, Moise agreed to pay Achille $57,500 for his share. An official notice was drawn up and back-dated to March 1, 1885. It read, in part:

> "The co-partnership heretofore existing between
> M. L. Wolff and A. Levy . . . was this day dissolved
> by mutual consent. Mr. M. L. Wolff having pur-
> chased the entire interest of Mr. A. Levy . . . (who)
> will assume all liabilities and collect all outstanding
> accounts . . . Thanking our patrons and the public
> for past favors, we ask for a continuance of the
> same for the new firm."[3]

The ordeal of the past year was over and Achille was a free man. He now proceeded with personal plans that would affect Ventura County and much of Southern California.

Many in the Hueneme financial community had realized that Achille's business dealings had for some time extended beyond the doors of Wolff and Levy. In fact, Achille's evolution from broker to banker is documented as occurring in 1882. This probably contributed to the strain in the relationship between him and Moise. Moise saw Achille's initiative in a different light from others. People were sure Hueneme was headed toward great commercial expansion and were overflowing with optimism. This was largely owing to the dynamic leadership, sponsorship, and energy of Senator Thomas R. Bard. Bard was a landowner and lawyer whose professed goal in life was to make Hueneme great. In 1882, success seemed assured when Bard was named Executor of the Estate of Thomas Scott, which comprised over half the prime land in the town. Once the vacant lots so prominent throughout Hueneme were developed into businesses and private homes, the sky would be the limit.

Unfortunately, this explosion in real estate so eagerly sought by Bard, Levy, and other speculators did not occur until 1888. The probate of Scott's enormous estate became immersed in the court system for nearly six years. All the Hueneme community could do was wait. Achille also had to be content with a smaller scale of business than he had originally planned. He spent these years buying barley, walnuts, apricots, and honey for the urban markets of Los Angeles and San Francisco. He also provided seed and loaned money for stock and farm implements to the local farmers.

In 1884, Achille's brother-in-law, Henry Levy, came to Hueneme from Paris. Well-educated at the prominent Lycee Henry IV in Paris, Henry Levy assumed much of the bookkeeping for Achille. From the outset, Henry was in charge of the sheep and cattle dealings of Achille's own brokerage firm even though he was only 18 years old. Achille thought highly of him and their relationship lasted a lifetime.

By 1885, Achille's record of good faith and astute business practices had begun to pay dividends. Mr. Charles J. Daily, manager of the enormous John Patterson Ranch, came to Achille and deposited most of his life savings. Daily, barely past 20 years of age at the time, deposited $480 with Achille. As this deposit was dated January 15, 1885, several conclusions may be drawn. Daily was not merely a "walk-in" customer. His association with the Patterson Ranch, one of the largest stock and agricultural enterprises in the county, meant Daily had advice from knowledgeable and experienced customers of A. Levy as a banker, no later than 1884. Second, the date of the deposit is well in advance of Achille's termination of the partnership of Wolff and Levy. That Daily heard about and looked up Achille so soon reveals that Achille was offering banking services before the firm of Wolff and Levy passed into history. Later Daily explained his life-long association with Achille:

"I used to consult with him on a great many things, and I still think he was the best businessman I ever knew. He was very nice and would do anything that would help me along that was within reason."[4]

This passage reveals the county-wide respect which Achille had already acquired by 1885. His calculated undertaking of a business separate from the Wolff and Levy partnership was already the source of great interest.

Soon after, in the spring of 1885, Levy commissioned a photographer to take a group picture of Lucy, Henry Levy and himself. As Lucy sits in a buggy at the reins of a well-proportioned trotting horse, Henry and Achille stand on the porch under a sign proclaiming, "A. Levy: Grain, Wool and Produce. Commission & Forwarding." Several items are worth noting. The set of screen doors guaranteed Achille's boast that: "There shall be no flies on me."[5] Also prominent are signs posted on the front windows stating his participation in the Royal Insurance Company, the Liverpool, London & Globe Insurance Company, and the North British Mercantile Association. While such impressive credentials added credibility and advertising to a largely English oriented clientele, the reason that caused patrons to pass through the new screen doors in ever-increasing numbers was Achille's approach to banking.

Palmyre, his second youngest daughter, gave insight into Achille's personal criteria for business clients when she stated:

> *"He always studied human nature, and in his quiet way liked to gamble on it to see if he'd guessed right. On the whole, he rarely failed and when he was right, there was always a twinkle in his eye when he told mother. He never bragged of what he had done and it was only upon his death that we knew how many he had helped."*[6]

A. Levy in front of brokerage. Seated in buggy is Lucy Levy.

T. Russell Carroll, who joined the bank as book-keeper and rose to vice president over a 50-year period recalled:

> *"Some of the methods of Achille Levy seem almost incredible when compared to the rigid banking practice as prescribed by law today. The so-called "character loan" was an early method used by many bankers, and Mr. Levy was a veritable disciple of the system. Essentially quite simple, it required only that the applicant be known to be of good character (and usually well liked) by the banker, in which case money in large sums and with no collateral would be loaned. However, if the person seeking money had thousands in collateral but was known to have character faults, not one cent was forthcoming. Surprisingly enough, this method of loaning purely on the basis of character resulted in but a few losses."* [7]

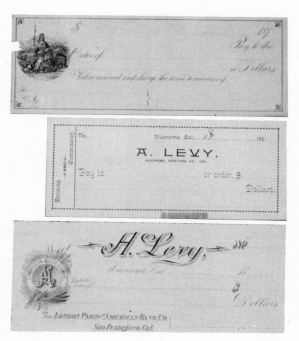

Bank checks

The last portion of the 19th century indulged private banking without the control of charter of state and federal agencies. Authorities on this wild financial era emphasize that private banking was only a success in those rare instances where the banker was capable, honest, and enjoyed the trust of his neighbors. The odds against such an appraisal were high, and Levy's success during this period is exceptional. Achille's renown as a man of character can be better appreciated when we acknowledge the basic distrust that farmers had of businessmen in general during this period. Perceived monopolies in the railroad and agricultural markets had driven prices so low in many areas that farmers were suffering greatly. They had to resort to such collective actions as the Grange Society (an agricultural union) and the often violent Populist Party.

Levy, who by 1890 clearly represented business, including railroad shipping, maintained his image as an honest broker. A contemporary newspaper made the statement: "His reputation for square dealing is as wide as the county and there is no businessman more popular among the farmers." (*Ventura Free Press*, December 1895, souvenir edition.)

The mechanics of Achille's banking practices were simple: A farmer who sold produce to him could choose not to collect the full sale price of his crop in cash at the time of delivery. Instead, the farmer trusted Achille as custodian of that portion of his cash which he did not require immediately. Levy provided the farmer with seed, cash for farm animals, equipment, staples, and general merchandise, then debited the account. When making his payment to other merchants, the same farmer issued a draft or check against his balance, with Achille as payer. Achille combined the knowledge of broker and banker. He offered the farmer an opportunity to market his harvest immediately and learn about new cash crop potential, all at one location: A. Levy's office.

Many farmers came to regard A. Levy, broker in agricultural supplies, as A. Levy, banker, due to their dependence on barley as a main cash crop. Barley was first planted in Pleasant Valley in the late 1860s by Christian and Ed Borchard. Barley was dry farmed, and the lack of irrigation meant that the farmers were at the mercy of the weather. It was not at all unusual for a man to depend on Achille for credit until a wet year came around. The barley, drawing a high price from the eastern breweries, in one season paid for three or four mediocre or disastrous years. As F. L. Fairbanks recalled:

> *"If a broker (such as Achille) agreed to carry a man until his crop was harvested, instead of giving him the full amount at the time (of request) he was given a checkbook. They usually had a verbal agreement as to what the man could draw on his banker for—not just anything, but something to keep going until harvest time. In the "barley days," if it was a dry year, the debt was carried over."*[8]

The barley harvest came during the months of August and September. Hueneme became a beehive of activity, with scores of spring wagons packed high with sacks of grain. Teams of horses, farmers, and children often stretched over a mile from the wharf. In good years, it was not unusual for such deliveries to take two or three days. In an average year, 300,000 sacks found their way to the warehouses. A poor year produced a third of that. It was a risky business, but not only for the barley farmer. Thomas R. Bard, who owned the wharf, and broker-bankers such as Achille also had a great deal at stake. Even if the yield was exceptional, the volume of shipping was calculated on a week-to-week basis and depended totally on the barley market in San Francisco. If too much Hueneme barley glutted the market, prices fell.

Achille Levy was at the very center of this activity. He was often both at the end of the lines of teams and wagons in Hueneme and on the telegraph lines to San Francisco. When a barley farmer finally reached the front of the long line of wagons and weighed in at the wharf scales, Achille was there to offer him the latest price for his produce. The farmer and broker

Local farmers at harvest time

made a verbal agreement on the total worth of the barley, and Achille gave his client a receipt for that amount. This transaction placed a note of credit in the farmer's hands, while the larger part of the balance would be placed on account with the Levy brokerage. If debts for groceries and farm equipment were outstanding, that amount would be deducted from the farmer's credit.

As mentioned earlier, the Hueneme (or seller's) end of the barley exchange was only half of Achille's responsibility. As a local resident and businessman, he had to offer the best possible quote on barley prices to his neighbors. This entailed their trust in his knowledge of the market. Being a member of the San Francisco Produce Exchange and Call Board was not window dressing. It was not unusual for Achille to spend over $200 per month with Western Union to keep on top of the market.

Although barley remained a staple Ventura

County product, its days as the main crop were numbered. Achille's contacts in the Midwest had informed him that new strains of barley were being developed nearer to the St. Louis breweries, and with lower freight costs, this barley would be available at a much lower price. Armed with this information, it was easier for Achille to convince the farmers that many breweries would quickly desert Ventura County, resulting in a lower overall price for Ventura grain.

Although the threat of depleted barley revenues inspired Achille to enter the lima bean business, his real motivation was the promise of increased profit potential in this new commodity. From the beginning, Achille shared his insight into lima beans with local Hueneme growers.

In 1870, a Peruvian vessel anchored off Santa Barbara. A farmer, Henry Lewis, became acquainted with the captain and was subsequently invited aboard for dinner. An unknown variety of bean was served. Lewis asked for some of the beans to take home and plant. Lima beans proved to be well suited to the coastal climate, and Lewis eventually had acres planted in them.

The success of lima beans on the Lewis Ranch in Carpinteria soon was noticed by farmers living north of the Santa Clara River, between Ventura and Montalvo. For the next 20 years, an increasing amount of this acreage was devoted to lima beans.

By 1887, Achille Levy had seen the success of lima bean plantings. In this year, the Southern Investment Company was formed as a cooperative to purchase lima bean seeds. In 1888, Levy's campaign to convince farmers south of the river took hold. Approximately 6,000 acres of the South River Plains were switched from grain to beans. Achille secured the seed from dealers all over the United States. The experiment was a success, and 4,500 tons (140,000 bags) were sent to the Hueneme wharf that year.

21

Although the 1888 season was a success, converting local farmers to the new crop was not easy. Barley raising, and its companion industry, hog raising (hogs were cheaply fed on barley mash) were firmly established. The barley farmers had done so well that they perceived any new crop to be a gamble. It took an innovative individual, and a gambler, to try Achille's new crop, lima beans.

After his success, Achille decided to build a market for lima beans throughout the United States, Mexico, and Europe. In 1887, the Southern Pacific Railroad laid a track north of the Santa Clara River on the Ventura side, making it possible to ship agricultural products by rail across the United States avoiding the long sea passage around Cape Horn. Because the major market for beans was in the Eastern cities, and transit by rail was faster and less damaging to perishables, the railroad increasingly became the only transportation necessary.

While Achille continued to do business with Bard and the Hueneme Wharf, the volume of his lima bean brokerage required that he soon look beyond the wharf to accommodate the volume of his new enterprise. By 1889, Achille was shipping beans from Hueneme to Denver, Chicago, Lincoln, Kansas City, and New York. In mid-1890, when local farmers had to make their choice between planting barley or beans, an article in the Hueneme paper indicated that beans were easier to handle and paid farmers 150 percent more than barley. The source of this information was Achille Levy. He also predicted that, given favorable weather conditions, a local farmer could produce 1,250 carloads of beans that year. Events soon demonstrated that the combination of advice and advertising had paid off.

In October of 1890, Achille sent almost 3,000 sacks of lima beans by steamer to San Pedro. From there they were transported by rail to Eastern cities. Twenty-two freight cars, two separate train loads,

The railroad arrives from Los Angeles

were filled with only lima beans. Both of these bean caravans, 10 cars of the Union Pacific and 12 cars of the Santa Fe, were draped with huge signs proclaiming: "Beans from A. Levy, Hueneme, California." A clever advertising ploy, this gesture made news and made Ventura County proud. After this extravaganza, Achille was known as the "Bean King" not only in Hueneme but throughout the entire county. He also gained national prominence at the Boston Board of Trade. A photograph of the two bean trains hung on the board room wall for decades, a tribute to an immigrant entrepreneur not yet 40 years old.

The years from 1888-1890 were critical to Achille's success. The estate of Thomas A. Scott, under litigation since 1882, was finally settled. As the local paper of December 13, 1888 explained, this resolution resulted in the public auction of 16,000 acres of the old La Colonia Rancho. Much of this ranch was centered in Hueneme and environs. The impact to Achille, and others who had invested so heavily in Hueneme's future, was both immediate and impressive. New houses, businesses, and farms were springing up in Hueneme during these years.

Financing for such growth was needed. Achille's new bank played a major role in providing the needed funds for this expansion.

It is noteworthy that there were only 90 customers who received the bulk of Achille's loans during the period from April 1885 through May of 1886. Almost *four of every seven dollars* A. Levy loaned in this formative stage went to 13 *individuals.* Some names are familiar county families, with C. A. Rice, Casper and John Borchard, J. F. Cummings, Simon Cohn, Jacob Maulhardt, J. B. Alvord, and Adolfo Camarillo being prominent. These customers gave Bank of A. Levy its initial solvency. Doing business from the start were the founders of other county families soon to become well established. The Petit, Hobson, Arneill, Saviers, Donlon, Lehmann, and Hill enterprises were only getting started in that year. During the next decade, they provided an ever-increasing business to Achille, both by loans and by selling him their crops.

Achille's clients were not limited to farming. Other customers included his old friends and associates in Hueneme. Benjamin H. Korts, the proprietor of a meat market; Rose and John McCoy, who invested in real estate; and Dr. William Reinhardt Livingston were among Achille's active patrons. A group of Chinese merchants regularly passed through his new screen doors. Six local families accounted for a large portion of his early loan business. Clients living in Santa Paula, Moorpark, Somis, Camarillo, and Oxnard were also important to Achille's business.

Achille's financial dealings with both small and large clients in these first years merit mention. Income made from interest on loans did not represent a large share of the new bank's financial growth. Total receipts for the first year's interest did not exceed $1,400 on nearly $54,000 worth of loans. It emerges that Achille's profits from banking in this and the subsequent years from 1886-1890 were not measured only in dollars and cents. Immediate profits depended heavily upon returns from his agricultural brokerage business, while long-term gains from loans were best

Adolfo Camarillo

measured by the trust that his patrons gradually placed in his services.

In 1888 and 1889, Achille's place in county finance greatly expanded. His success at converting local farmers to lima beans during 1888 had gained the attention and respect of Thomas Bard. Early in 1889, he suggested to Levy and other merchants of Hueneme that their interests would best be served by incorporating in a local bank. This bank, the Bank of Hueneme, would serve the farmers and merchants south of Ventura. Bard had prior banking experience as the first President of the Bank of Ventura, the first organized in the county, in 1874. The only other bank in the county was the Bank of William Collins and Sons, founded in Ventura during the fall of 1887. There clearly was a need for a Hueneme bank, as the wharf business of barley and beans had grown very large, and fording the Santa Clara River made regular banking trips to Ventura difficult.

To solve this problem, Bard called together Achille, Moise Wolff, and five other leading citizens, and convinced them to join him in the incorporation of the Bank of Hueneme on February 21, 1889. Achille was very active in this endeavor from the start. On April 4, 1889, he was elected Vice President of the new institution, with Bard as President. The bank was capitalized with $100,000, with Bard holding 200 shares at $100 apiece. Other major stockholders, including Levy, each bought 50 shares at $100 apiece, representing a total investment of $5,000 each.

Achille was responsible for the construction of the building that housed the newly formed Bank of Hueneme. In a town noted for muddy streets, it was the first brick building and also featured the city's first cement sidewalks. Scheduled to open on August 1, 1889, the Bank of Hueneme actually began doing business five days later.

Hueneme trolley

Even within the formal structure of the Bank of Hueneme, Achille was able to conduct business as he saw fit. He continued to operate his own brokerage with bank funds and personal business assets, shifting money back and forth to mutual benefit. Industry standards for banking were not as yet in place so Levy utilized many of his own business practices at the Bank of Hueneme, including the issuing of his own Bank of Hueneme checkbooks to reliable farmers. The bank debited these checks against Levy's personal account. Often there were substantial overdrafts on which Achille paid nine percent interest. F. L. Fairbanks, who worked as a teller in the Bank of Hueneme for many years, recalled the overdrafts sometimes reached more than $50,000. Although Achille had to pay his nine percent per annum on a monthly basis on over-drafts of any size, Fairbanks states:

> *"You can be sure that Levy was saving money or he would not have done it. I think his credit was such that he could have had anything he wanted from London, Paris and American Bank Ltd., in San Francisco, his correspondent bank."*[9]

A. Levy (second from right) in front of brokerage

Other practices of such early banks are worth noting. No paper money or pennies were used. Gold and silver were given to customers upon withdrawal, usually on a half and half basis. This procedure often led to problems if the amount was high, as the coins were heavy.

Without the convenience of pennies, banks used a method termed "breakage," based on the nickel. If a balance was two cents or less, the bank kept the breakage. If three cents or more, it was given to the customer.

Another difference between early and modern banking practices is the method of customer identification. As Fairbanks noted, a foreign-born farmer with no formal education got a loan to buy land using this procedure:

> "I got out a signature card and asked him to write his name. To my surprise it seemed that he couldn't write his name, but he explained to me, that everyone else who couldn't write always made a little cross, but that he would make a little round "o" for his mark, and we would know he made it. He later became one of the county's most substantial farmers." [10]

The year of 1890 was a watershed in American history. Across the country and in Ventura, farmers were doing poorly. Expectations for the 1880s had been frustrated by lower prices on agricultural goods. This frustration was reflected in demands for a return to the silver standard, which meant easier credit terms than with the existing gold standard. This was done in the hope of avoiding the foreclosures on farms that were prevalent in the late 1880s.

The desperate situation brought forth an unprecedented amount of action in the 1890 national elections. The Grange Society, comprised of local groups of farmers cooperating with a regional political leadership, and the Populist Party voiced the frustration of dissatisfied farmers and the urban working class. These groups identified government and "big business," especially the railroad, meat packing, and agricultural brokers, as members of a large monopolistic establishment which exploited the farmer and worker. Sympathetic political writers and cartoonists such as Upton Sinclair and Thomas Nast were merciless in their depiction of big business. Quite prominent in characterizations of politicians, businessmen, and bankers was the hog. A familiar sight to most farmers, this slothful and gluttonous beast represented their conception of what was wrong with America. Not surprisingly, this distrust was especially focused on bankers.

Achille escaped this widespread condemnation that was so prevalent. Locals considered him an honest man and trusted his commission and brokerage firm, as well as the Bank of Hueneme. Only a person with great integrity would have been trusted to keep the large sums of money given to him by hard-working farmers.

Achille had labored hard for this trust. By 1890, he was very well known in the community. Only 37, his reputation was already widely established. He had successfully encouraged many farmers to switch from barley to beans, saving many local farmers from the fate of ever-diminishing returns growing so common throughout the country. They were grateful. Levy's partnership with Thomas Bard and the Hueneme Wharf Company also played an important part in his reputation, as this relationship allowed him to quote the lowest possible shipping rates. The advent of the Southern Pacific Railroad north of the river in 1887 had not affected his business. Bard and Levy worked with the Santa Fe system's subsidiary, California Southern Railway, which had an eastbound route from its ocean terminals. This let Bard quote shipping rates that included storage and connecting water freight charges. Achille was the major patron of this route, and, as such, forced the monopoly-prone

29

Southern Pacific Railroad to provide reasonable fares throughout the county. Farmers were thus spared the high freight rates prevalent throughout California, and Achille gained the respect and gratitude of his Ventura clientele.

Although his reputation served him well, it was only part of the success Achille enjoyed in 1890. His status as a member of the local Hueneme community kept him visible and accessible, which was important in an era when most bankers were not trusted.

Hueneme had only four main streets at the time, Market, Broad, Main, and Fourth. Achille's modest house on Main Street placed him in the center of the residential and business section. Most of the bank's early customers were his neighbors, and he socialized with them regularly. Although he owned more spacious and private lots nearby, he and Lucy remained on Main Street until they moved to Oxnard in 1912. Their ten acre plot just outside of town, which many thought would be the site of an estate, was devoted to Achille's own experiments in agriculture.

The Levy family had, by this time, grown to six. In addition to Achille's and Lucy's community involvement, they were busy raising four children, Anna, Palmyre, Julia, and their son, Joseph.

Achille was further distinguished from the prototype banker of the era by his personality and personal approach to customers. His role in Ventura County affairs extended beyond that of a local businessman and banker. In addition to his early service as postmaster, he was elected to the Hueneme School Board in 1890 and served in this capacity for many years. (*Hueneme Herald*, June 5, 1890). The Hueneme Club, a business and social organization similar to a current-day chamber of commerce, counted him as a member. Perhaps his greatest contribution, however, came as being Hueneme's delegate to the County Board of Supervisors. He held this position during the period of time the Santa Clara River bridge project was under debate. *(Hueneme Herald*, February 6, 1890). Achille, with other prominent citizens, was influential in assuring the construction of the bridge.

The Santa Clara River had long been a most dangerous natural barrier to cross, and a communications barrier between the north and south of Ventura County. Many persons, animals, and possessions were lost in its quicksand and seasonal flooding. On November 22, 1888, two children were drowned when their family wagon fell into a hole while crossing. This tragedy was widely reported in Ventura County, and a furor arose over the need and cost for a bridge. Similar occurrences followed, but nothing was done. During February of 1890, the *Hueneme Herald* reported that the Board of Supervisors had met to discuss the problem, and Achille took an active role, speaking in favor of the bridge. By a vote of 17 to 4, it was decided to get estimates for a bridge, both at the Saticoy and Lime Kiln (now Montalvo) crossings. The problem remained until 1898, when the efforts of Achille and other advocates were at last rewarded. The bridge was important for safety reasons, and provided a link between Hueneme and the outside world as well. Achille and other Hueneme school trustees, in honor of the occasion, decided to close school and allow the children to attend the bridge dedication ceremonies.

Achille's efforts toward agricultural, mercantile, and social welfare did not pass unnoticed by Ventura County's political leaders. On January 23, 1890, the *Hueneme Herald* reported that Levy was summoned to be a candidate for the nomination on the Republican ticket for the District Assembly. During the next few months, Achille was very active in state-wide politics, with numerous members of the Republican Party proposing his candidacy. The *Ventura Vidette* of February 5, 1890, repeated the possibility of Achille's political baptism by stating that he was a viable candidate for State Assembly. After this initial flurry, references to his projected campaign became scarce. On March 22, 1890, the *Ventura Free Press* said:

A. *Levy inspecting hogs in his own backyard*

*"We are occasionally asked whom the Republicans
propose nominating for the various county offices
this year. We can answer that in about five months
from this date, we propose letting the Republican
nominating convention decide that matter, and their
choice is likely to be our choice. They have a large
number of good men to draw from and we have no
fears but they will place the right men on the ticket
and that they will be elected. There is plenty of
time to name candidates five or six months hence."*

Several explanations exist for the absence of continued support for Achille as an Assembly candidate.
One possibility is that he and Senator Bard had come
to a parting of the ways. Whether the scarcity of
references to Levy in Bard's political correspondence
reflected a difference in political opinion, or perhaps
was the result of Levy's increasing independence in
economic ventures (i.e., his use of the railroad instead
of Bard's wharf), is uncertain. In any event, without
Bard's active support, Achille had no chance of attain-
ing political office. Another explanation for Achille's
name having been withdrawn is that by the spring of
1890, he was deeply involved in a number of agricul-

tural enterprises. Assembly office would have meant residency in Sacramento, with prolonged absences from Hueneme. Achille's long-term financial and personal investment, in an area he had done much to create, was an important consideration, along with the priority he had always placed on the welfare of his family. For Achille, moving from the secure haven of Hueneme was a most unwelcome prospect.

Whatever the reason, by the summer of 1890, Achille retired as an Assembly candidate. However, his interest in politics had not waned. On June 12, 1890, he was listed in Bard's papers as a member of the Republican nominating committee for Congressional Candidates from Ventura County. The following month, his new role in Republican politics found him named as a delegate to the state nominating convention.

In 1890, Ventura County had only 9,000 citizens. Thirty percent lived south of the Santa Clara River. Most were farmers who looked to Hueneme as their market. Achille Levy had, in four years, played a major role in putting Hueneme on the national financial map. Under favorable weather conditions, Ventura County could produce 12,500 railroad cars of beans. Achille worked hard toward increasing production. As he encouraged lima bean farming south of the river, he anticipated an increase in profits. An acre of land, under barley production, yielded $20 per acre. It would now net a lima bean farmer $50 per acre, with only slightly higher production cost. (*Hueneme Herald,* April 24, June 5, and June 26, 1890.) The optimism shared by Achille and local farmers was widespread. Local newspapers chided their southern neighbors:

> *"It is stated that a good quality of whiskey can be made from the beans. Probably this accounts for Ventura's 40,000 acres of Boston's Delight [i.e. beans]."* (Ventura Free Press, *March 25, 1890.*)

The humor reflected social snobbery, but Achille's accomplishments certainly gained notice.

Chapter II

The Founding of Bank of
A. Levy

Both business and agricultural communities in
the town of Hueneme shared the feeling of optimism
during the 1890s, and for good reason. The *Ventura
Vidette* gave several reasons on March 23, 1890:

> *"Hueneme is noticeably improved within the last
> two years. A beautiful and commodious school
> house has been built, several new dwellings and
> others improved, a bank established, a new church
> and so forth. The town has a good farming country
> in back of it, and as the grain shipping port for all
> points east and south of the Santa Clara [it must
> succeed]."*

Until 1900, the Hueneme harbor area was the
most vital factor in the growth of Ventura County. A
map of the region during this era clearly shows that
roads from the surrounding countryside led to the
Port of Hueneme.

In July of 1891, Achille Levy was so confident
that he predicted that an unprecedented $100,000
worth of agricultural products would be produced on
the south side of the Santa Clara River. (*Hueneme
Herald*, July 30, 1891). This optimistic estimate was
based on the market price for beans of five cents per
pound, achieved in 1890. There was no reason to
believe that next year's market would offer any less.
The future of local agriculture looked most promising.
A technological innovation of immediate relevance to
the local farmers was a bean planter. Patented by Scott
Saviers, a local farmer-machinist, the machine could

Ventura County, circa 1900

be used by bean growers worldwide. C. J. Daily, prominent manager of the Patterson Ranch, found it pleasingly necessary to build his own granaries due to Hueneme's booming business.

Newspapers in both Hueneme and Ventura reflected the excitement over growth. The barley and bean trade promised ever-increasing incomes. Optimistic moods were clearly shown in the enthusiasm for new buildings. Many new homes were built with Northern pine and redwood brought in by steamers. A new two-story school was built, complete with elaborate Victorian ornamentation, and a belfry to chime students to class. Churches sprang up all over town, thanks to the charity of Thomas R. Bard.

An example of these well-constructed buildings was the Presbyterian Church, dedicated September 11, 1892. Forsaking traditional church architecture, this impressive edifice combined civic involvement with its function as a chapel. Entering the church through the covered porch and sitting rooms, the first impression was that of being in a graceful private residence. Such architecture illustrates the duality of Hueneme life during this era, religious but also concerned with the social graces.

Many other examples exist of the building boom that Hueneme experienced in the 1890s. A new post office, sharing quarters with a new telephone company, was completed in late 1893. Gone were the days when the post office was conducted as a side-line duty by local merchants.

Along with Hueneme's increasing financial status came tourism and the construction of the elaborate Seaside Hotel. By 1893, the tourist trade had showed substantial promise and thousands of dollars were spent to meet the desires of inland farmers and businessmen looking for a few days' vacation by the sea. Other developments improved the quality of life in Hueneme, such as new sidewalks along the much traveled route between the B. Korts department/ grocery store and the Seaside Hotel.

All of these improvements in farming and build-

A. Levy on couch

ing relied on the availability of water, the most necessary element to progress in Southern California. In Hueneme, artesian springs were tapped with relative ease in many locations. Agriculture was an obvious beneficiary of such easy access to water. Other benefits abounded. Hot and dusty days became less oppressive as water was sprinkled on local roads by horse-drawn tanks.

Even though water was abundant, it was not enough to douse the fire that destroyed Hueneme's business district on March 22, 1894. R. B. Haydock, Schoolmaster and later superintendent of schools, recounted:

> "The 'big fire' in Hueneme occurred some time after midnight. It started in the store of Gilger and Waterman, swept through the Wolff and Lehman store [the largest mercantile establishment in the county], the Bank of Hueneme and the wharf office just to the rear. It was thought that the wharfinger's [Wharf manager's] residence, about 25 feet from the wharf office, might be saved. There was no fire fighting apparatus in town and pressure from the artesian wells was not strong enough to reach the roof. Some of us climbed a ladder to the roof while others passed up buckets of water. In a short time, the roof became wet and slippery, and down I skidded over the awning above the porch. Louis Ludekens [a local merchant] was filling a bucket of water from a hydrant and I landed squarely on his shoulders, driving him to the ground. Fortunately, there was a thick growth of calla lilies around the hydrant and Louis was not hurt." (Hueneme Herald, March 22, 1894.)

The center of Hueneme was gutted. Although many principal business buildings were destroyed, vital warehouses survived. Six warehouses on the wharf, which were filled with grain and beans at the time, were saved.

Personally, Thomas R. Bard, the owner of

the wharf and the warehouses, was not so lucky. ". . . Nothing remains but the brick vaults of the bank and those of T. R. Bard. Many papers and documents in the office of Bard were destroyed and the loss is a most serious one to him." (*Hueneme Herald*, March 22, 1894.) The total loss in the fire was placed at $75,000. Bard carried insurance for only half that amount.

Within a year, the essential vitality of Hueneme business was re-established. Insurance claims were paid and private capital rallied to rebuild the business community, this time in brick, rather than wood. Plans were made for the construction of a new bank building and office building for the wharf company, both of which were to be made of brick. T. R. Bard had learned his lesson, as he contracted for a brick vault to house his personal books, maps, and other valuables.

Innovations in business continued. Achille increasingly looked to his brother-in-law, Henry Levy, for assistance. As mentioned earlier, Henry came to Hueneme in 1884 and, from the outset, had worked for Achille in his brokerage. As he was only 18 years old, most of his time was spent behind the counter, as an apprentice bookkeeper. When Wolff bought out Achille in 1885, Henry went along with his brother-in-law, occupying the same low-profile position in Levy's new enterprise.

Well into the 1890s, Achille himself performed much of the field work and customer contact of the new business. During the harvest season, Achille manned the wharf scales. Often he worked 12-to 14-hour days. The barley and bean wagons formed a single file line nearly two miles long.

Long days for Achille led to a more visible and significant role for Henry. By 1891, he was handling the sheep, swine, and cattle business of the firm. In addition, he was responsible for a portion of its general merchandising. Henry was a very hard worker.

Achille grew increasingly aware of Henry's contribution to the business. In February of 1900, Achille planned an extended family vacation to France, including reunions with relatives. The trip lasted almost a year and a half. Before Achille left, in recognition of the respect given to Henry by the local farmers, he published, in the *Hueneme Herald*, a notice of partnership with his 34-year-old brother-in-law. Henry received a one-third working interest in Achille's brokerage firm. From this time forward, the firm was officially known as A & H Levy Company, with Achille as the Senior Partner. Business details attended to, Achille left the country knowing that affairs would be well-handled by Henry.

Henry's interests occasionally drew him out of the brokerage house. He loved trotting horses and, with Leon Lehmann, began one of the first race tracks in Ventura. Lehmann, another Alsatian immigrant and cousin of Achille, was a young and vibrant European gentleman longing to bring a bit of old-world culture and excitement to Ventura County. Henry's early involvement as secretary of the race track and horse owner made him a public figure, and as such, enhanced his future career.

President McKinley in Ventura County, 1901

The race track was a popular meeting place, though it kept an irregular schedule. Considered to be the best in the county, it frequently featured horses from Santa Paula, Hueneme, and Ventura. The track was close to town, with a nearby restaurant providing refreshments to the spectators.

During these years, professional businessmen met socially at both fraternal orders and private clubs. In Hueneme, the first fraternal organization was the Ancient Order of United Workmen (AOUW), founded in the 1880s. Achille was a member of this society, and received the benefits of association with other leading businessmen in the community.

Other fraternal and social clubs soon started to satisfy the interests of Hueneme society. One of the first of these was the Hueneme Club. A strictly local club, it served to keep the businessmen and professional people of Hueneme aware of common interest

Young Joe Levy with shotgun

issues. A more significant organization, however, was founded in 1892. The Hueneme Lodge of Free and Accepted Masons had as its founding treasurer,

Achille's former partner, Moise Wolff. Achille was very active in Freemasonry, serving as Treasurer to the Hueneme and Oxnard lodges for 15 years. On August 21, 1892, Achille's long service was recognized and he was elevated to the rank of a master.

Committed to social service and financial support for charities within the community, the Masons were a focus for social activity. As an historian of local Masonic history said:

> *"Those were the halcyon days of old Hueneme, when merchant princes of the day vied with each other in giving banquets and entertainments-Lucullian affairs in Hueneme Lodge still spoken of with awe by old timers who attended them, and San Buenaventura had to at least try to keep up with her brilliant daughter."* [11]

The Hueneme Lodge continued to thrive through the 1890s. On the day after Christmas, 1895, Achille was once again elected treasurer to the lodge. Four years later, the group traveled to San Buenaventura for the dedication of the new Masonic Hall, still located at the junction of California and Santa Clara streets. A new Masonic Temple opened in Oxnard in September of 1901. Henry Levy's participation as Grand Master highlighted the shift of both business and society from Hueneme to Oxnard.

Political activity provided a touch-stone of community involvement. While Achille no longer aspired to political office, he and others among the mercantile and professional community actively participated in the political dialogue. On September 10, 1896, Claus Spreckles, the sugar beet entrepreneur of Northern California, visited Hueneme. He was a Democrat and a strong supporter of William Jennings Bryan, McKinley's rival for the Presidency. A staunch McKinley Republican, Achille served as a Hueneme delegate to the Republican county conventions of both 1896 and 1898, and met with Spreckles. Levy and Spreckles were touted by the local press as the Bean and Sugar Kings, respectively.

There were two other social organizations in Hueneme, perhaps best described as "gentlemen's clubs." One met every month or so and was generally known as the "bachelor's club." The form of recreation for members such as Joe Donlon, I. M. Poggi, and Henry Levy has not been recorded. From time to time

Levy family in Hueneme

in the local newspaper appeared accounts of marathon poker games. At one such meeting in 1899, the members requested the aid of their married friends in helping them find appropriate mates. Achille was made chairman of the newly formed Matrimonial Bureau, and was a success at this endeavor. He found wives for both Donlon and Poggi. Henry Levy, however, remained a bachelor until 1912.

Another recreational fraternity was the Hueneme Duck Club. Organized in the late 1890s, this group honed its shooting skills on the many ducks and geese populating the marshes south and west of present-day Oxnard. While Achille did not actively participate in hunting, Henry and Achille's son, Joe, were avid sportsmen in this group.

Events such as the Ventura County Fair in the city of Ventura, drew great enthusiasm and participation from county residents. Among the active participants was Lucy Levy. The Fair appears to have been her first major step into community affairs. At the first of the gatherings, Lucy displayed her expertise in culinary art, taking charge of the cooking entries.

News spread by word of mouth throughout the county, and the attendance signaled that the Fair was a success. Twelve hundred people attended the first day, 1,600 the second and 2,300 the third. The 1891 population of all Ventura County totaled not much more than this. In 1895, the town again assumed responsibility for this event, with Lucy acting as co-chairwoman for the Department of Flowers and Plants.

"Modern" technology had a significant impact on Hueneme, as seen in a statement from the *Hueneme Herald:*

> *"Horse power appears to be in demand here. Besides Borchard's horse powered sausage machine, the Reese Brothers have rigged up a machine for mixing mortar in the same way."* [12]

Road from Santa Barbara to Ventura County

The latter innovation was especially significant in the wake of the fire that had destroyed the Hueneme business district. Brick buildings had been built to replace the wooden ones that had been destroyed. The motor offered a fast and reasonable source of mortar.

In 1897, scores of people attended the exhibition of the first phonograph in Hueneme, which caused

A. Levy on porch

quite a sensation. At the Seaside Hotel, there were music programs. Promoters made a healthy profit, especially when spectators were moved to purchase a phonograph.

Another machine achieving great popularity during these years was the bicycle. Bicyclists were everywhere. The number of bicyclists in 1899 is hinted at by the *Herald's* following report:

> *"There is still agitation for a bicycle path from Hueneme to Oxnard and several wheelmen of this locality are heartily in favor of it."* (Hueneme Herald, *March 16, 1899.*)

Not all Hueneme residents took to their bikes, however.

*"Tom Clark, the 85-year-old popular horseman,
received a bicycle as a prize from the San Francisco
Examiner and doesn't know what to do with the
darn thing."* (Hueneme Herald, *August 8, 1901.)*

While the phonograph and bicycle were striking
examples of technology, the telegraph was far and
away a more profound innovation for business. In
November of 1895, Achille's telegraph bill of $241
reflected the impact of this technology. His bill was
more than that of the rest of Hueneme combined.
Efficiency and utilization of technology contributed to
Achille's success.

Between 1890 and 1902, Achille was still primarily
involved in the brokerage business. He was not alone
in this endeavor. Moise Wolff and Leon Lehmann of
Hueneme, Simon Cohn of El Rio, and Abraham
Bernheim of Ventura were also agricultural brokers.
What distinguished Achille from these other brokers
was his ever-increasing involvement in banking. By
1895, Achille operated a bank under his own name. It
fronted on Main Street, Hueneme, next to the mercantile store of Lehmann and Waterman and the hotel
owned by a good friend of Levy's, Dr. Benjamin Korts.

Banking was difficult in the mid 1890s. Times
were tough for farmers. Low rainfall failed to supply
the minimal moisture needed for beans or barley.
More than ever, Achille had to depend upon his
personal knowledge to determine if a man had what
it took to work against the forces of nature.

The list of farmers carried over by Achille during
this period is a large catalog of trust. Some were modest,
just beginning their career and in need of 100 percent
financing. If, as was the case of Antoine Baptiste in
1891, they agreed to experiment with lima beans on
their property, Achille loaned them the money for
more than one year without collateral or interest. The
drought, in many cases, persisted, and Achille's com-

mitment to the dry farmers had to endure until the rains came.

While the dry years of the 1890s presented a real challenge to farmers throughout Ventura County, their efforts were rewarded. With the support of Achille and other local brokers, the number of acres planted increased each year. In 1895, the total crop shipped from the Hueneme wharf amounted to 26,000 tons, 60 percent of which were limas. Farmers learned that the lima bean crop, more than any other, distributed the most money in wages and required the greatest warehouse capacity. The value of the 1895 bean crop was estimated at $1.1 million. Achille, among other experts, agreed that one half of the arable land for bean culture had yet to be used. The 1895 yield was nearly 700,000 sacks of lima beans. Many people thought that production could reach one million sacks per year. This large scale of productivity created problems of surplus. The bean producers realized that while there was no danger of competition in limas from other parts of California, the increased acreage was yielding such enormous crops that Eastern markets were glutted. Prices became so low (from 5 cents per pound in 1890 to 2½ cents per pound in 1895) that many Ventura county bean farmers became worried.

In mid-1895, a small but significant number of bean growers convinced themselves that the current low price for limas did not reflect the actual demand of the marketplace. In July, they took action and formed an association for the marketing of their limas. As time passed, however, the 2½ cents price did not change. It became apparent that the large surplus of beans might not sell. At that point, Achille, whom the growers had engaged (among others) as a selling agent, offered to buy the extra beans out of his own pocket. The association directors accepted his offer, and the association voted to cease operations, as their experiment had failed.

However, they began to distrust what had happened and thoughts of conspiracy echoed throughout the county. Still, Populist farmers were very suspicious of "business." The farmers' fears were well expressed in an alleged exposé written some years later by the Populist, Lee Bernard McConville. McConville's rather impassioned and seemingly factual article about Achille was flawed on many points. Achille was falsely linked to a man named J. K. Armsby, who was an unscrupulous speculator. Achille did all he could to disavow any association with this Chicago-based dealer.

Armsby's agent in Ventura County was Frank E. Barnard. In the late summer of 1895, members of the Lima Bean Association were starting to get nervous about the large surplus of unsold beans. Barnard issued statements to both the *Hueneme Herald* and *Ventura Free Press* denying that Armsby & Company had been offering 2½ cents per pound for beans and then selling them for the same amount, thereby breaking the market. This statement was challenged by Levy, as well as Moise Wolff, Leon Lehmann, and a number of other shippers and brokers from the Los Angeles area. The matter did not rest there, as Achille was angered by Barnard's claims. In a personal "Reply to F. E. Barnard" addressed to the editor of the *Herald*, he issued a public challenge to prove that Armsby had indeed sold 1895 beans at 2½ cents per pound. Barnard chose not to take Achille up on this challenge, as no further mention of the matter appears in the *Herald* or *Free Press*.

Although the Populist McConville chose to overlook Achille's forceful repudiation of Armsby's tactics, the trust shown in Achille in subsequent years by Ventura County farmers spoke for itself.

People in the county recognized that Achille's success came not from manipulation, but from business acumen. Small farmers financed by Achille in these years did quite well in limas. Charles Daily, manager of the Patterson Ranch, wanted to go out on his own and was unable to afford a threshing machine.

"When the beans were ripe . . . we tramped them out with horses and cleaned them by hand. I hauled them down to Hueneme and sold them to Mr. Levy, and had enough money to pay him off (for Levy's one percent interest loan on seed and property mortgage). In other words, I paid in three months what I thought would take me three years." [13]

His brother, Wendell Daily, experienced a similar success story when he purchased 200 acres of land with virtually no capital. The Daily brothers, who came to Hueneme from the East, demonstrated to Achille that hard work habits equaled good collateral. This trust was the basis of his banking success in the next century as well.

Achille could afford to carry small farmers because of his successful opening of new lima markets. In 1891 and 1892, he found large-quantity buyers in South America and Mexico. At the Chicago World's Fair in 1893, his expertise in advertising the bean was recognized by an award proclaiming Achille's display of a bean pagoda as one of the best bean exhibits at the Fair. His efforts brought rewards from the international marketplace, and the result was felt in Hueneme. Achille was not only profiting from the wholesale bean market, but he also had the business of East Coast bean seed agencies. He could dispose of surplus beans when the wholesale market was weak.

Achille was successful in other agricultural commerce. His interests became increasingly diverse. In October of 1895, Achille negotiated the largest purchase of apricots ever transacted in the county. Levy enterprises were not limited to local crops nor to Hueneme shipping. Diverse dealings included transporting a carload of prunes to Chatsworth, and dealing in sheep, both for their wool and meat.

A unique investment of Achille's was a stallion. Achille, along with the Borchards, Maulhardts, Leon Lehmann, Adolfo Camarillo, and others, invested $8,000 for the horse. Achille was apparently quite knowledgeable about horses and was often asked to serve as clerk at horse auctions. Charles Daily recalls:

"The people who bought [the horses] paid Mr. Levy in cash or check, or gave him a C-note. He knew everyone, so he was capable of taking notes from those who were not able or were not in the habit of paying cash. Later he collected everything so we did not lose a dollar on the sale of those horses." [14]

Authoritative proof of Achille's success in the 1890s was his tax bill. In that era, few items escaped publication. In 1895, readers of the *Herald* were informed:

"The two largest checks [in the county] in payment of taxes were from the Collins and Sons, Bank of Ventura, for $5,240.23 and the Bank of A. Levy for $5,083.70." (November 28, 1895.)

This news was significant for two reasons: it demonstrated Achille's financial success; and, for the first time, the name "Bank of A. Levy" appeared in print.

Achille's knowledge of county residents was enormous. His continued success relied upon his knowledge of the area's people and agriculture. Even when the demands of business required more of his time, he still greeted customers with the familiar refrain, "Sit down, let's talk awhile." His personal interest in the welfare and doings of his clientele continued to extend beyond matters of business throughout Achille's life.

Achille was not content to sit in his office and let agents do his field work. He had a great advantage over most other brokers due to his energetic and methodical surveys of the countryside. His detailed and accurate appraisals allowed Achille to extend credit without problems. An industrious farmer did not have to worry about being overdrawn, even in dry years.

Achille's brokerage and banking business was documented in a pocket-sized notebook that he carried from 1897 to 1899. He recorded his daily activities in the field, categorizing the factors that he deemed important in ascertaining an individual's credit worthiness.

In the fall of 1897, he made a number of trips out to Piru and Simi Valley to buy honey. He made a list of the best producers and, after visiting each, noted the prices that he offered them for their honey. Achille calculated the purchases on the spot, paying for them at the time of the visit. The transactions were registered as "took on myself," meaning that they had come out of his personal account. When buying such perishable items as walnuts, Achille noted that a certain quantity was not good and would indicate the reason. Farmers knew he was an agricultural expert, and few attempted to deceive him.

These notebooks are also useful in refuting one of the most damaging accusations leveled against Achille by the Populists' critique of his "speculation and manipulation" of lima bean prices. In them are recorded the prices paid for produce during October of 1899. These records were for Achille's eyes only, and not contrived for judgment. From the outset of the month, when local farmers Edward Gisler, and Johannes Diedrich, sold their beans at about 3.9 cents per pound; until the end of October when other farmers received in excess of 4.5 cents per pound, there are no variations from a steady upturn in price. No special accommodations were made for large growers, and no evidence of consideration for any bean producer or broker is noted. The market dictated what Achille offered.

The products that Achille acquired were either shipped immediately to Hueneme or stored in warehouses located in Somis, Santa Paula, Saticoy, Montalvo, Oxnard, and Ventura. In 1897, the bulk of Achille's east valley produce was stored and shipped through Saticoy. By 1899, he already had rerouted his purchases to the "town of the future," Oxnard.

Considerable capital was required to finance his brokerage and initial banking endeavors during the 1890s. Achille looked beyond Ventura County for advertising and investments. As a part of his investment portfolio, Achille had European bonds, principally in France and Germany. While the amounts were not high enough to call him an international banker, he did realize a steady income from foreign holdings. When World War I caused economic distress in Europe, Achille decided to withdraw his money from foreign depositories. The total amount of such investments was approximately $7,000.

Achille continued to keep the bulk of his investments in the local economy throughout the 1890s. Thereafter, he concentrated his stock buying in Ventura County, other parts of California, and the western states. While sentiment and some profit involved him in foreign investments, the returns of his Hueneme interests were quite considerable and more under his control.

In 1895, events of which Achille had no foresight or ability to control were beginning to change the future of Hueneme and Ventura County. Henry Oxnard, the most dynamic member of a prestigious and wealthy family of sugar beet planters and refiners, was looking for new territory to develop. Already having established a profitable sugar beet enterprise in Louisiana, Henry and his brothers knew the potential of their product. During the early 1890s, they went on to establish three other factories, the last of which was in Chino, California. In 1895, Albert Maulhardt of Ventura County entered the picture. Maulhardt had a 640-acre ranch about two miles south of present-day Oxnard, as well as some land near Camarillo. He was known to his contemporaries as an "idea man."

A close friend and neighbor, Henry Borchard, was using stock sugar beets as cattle feed during the mid 1890s. Maulhardt had the foresight to invite the field representative of Henry Oxnard's Chino factory to Montalvo to perform an analysis of the local soils and sugar content of Borchard's 1895 crop. While Borchard's stock beets did not contain quite enough sugar for production, the soil was promising. Maulhardt was so convincing in his arguments for sugar beet production that the Chino representative sent down sufficient hybrid beet seeds for the 1896 plantings. Borchard, Maulhardt, and a few other farmers were willing to experiment.

Achille played an active role in Albert Maulhardt's sugar beet project. As the dealer for the Chino seeds, he placed advertisements in the *Hueneme Herald* which announced that he had received beet seed and planters from Chino. He requested that farmers get the seed and try it. One who did was the father of Jessie Gill, who recalled Levy's part in testing the soil for beet production. Its alkali content would prove even more beneficial to beets than beans.

Analysis of the 1896 crop showed over 20 percent saccharine (sugar), roughly twice as high as necessary for profitable production. Maulhardt was so pleased with these results that, upon learning that Henry Oxnard was in San Francisco, he traveled there and presented a case for sugar beet production and processing in Ventura County. Maulhardt was a most convincing advocate for his ideas, and this trip proved no exception. Oxnard let out sugar beet contracts to Ventura farmers for over 1,000 acres in 1897. Their great success—some yields averaging over 30 percent sac-

Oxnard sugar beet plant

charine—guaranteed that any plant that the Oxnards might build in Ventura County would be profitable.

A question remained as to where the plant was to be built. Initial efforts to place it near the wharf in Hueneme failed, principally owing to the opposition of Thomas R. Bard, the largest landowner in that area. Senator Bard did not care to see this pleasant and gentle village by the sea turned into a factory town, cheapened by an onslaught of unskilled and uncultured sugar beet workers.

Bard's refusal meant the only logical alternative for the plant was near the site of sugar beet production. This area consisted of approximately 100 acres amidst the open fields just north of Wooley Road and east of Saviers Road. Maulhardt, along with Levy, Leon Lehmann, J. E. Borchard, E. P. Foster, and others, persuaded and assisted local farmers in underwriting the cost of buying this land from Thomas A. Rice.

During 1897, there was considerable negotiation on terms for the $2 million factory proposed by the Oxnards. Local farmers had to pledge 10,000 acres to beets in 1898 and 20,000 acres for five years thereafter. They also had to donate land for the Southern Pacific Railroad to build a spur to the site. Construction began in November of 1897 and over the course of the next two years, the Oxnards pledged to spend a total of $6 million on plant construction, beet contracts, and labor. This was an unprecedented scale of growth in Ventura County, and a great impact was felt immediately.

A group of present-day Ventura families trace their origins to the men who came to staff the plant. Some of the chemists, mechanics, and operators came from as far away as Louisiana. For the most part, this group consisted of sugar chemists who had received their training in Germany and were "imported" by the Oxnards to practice their trade in America. Some came from the New Orleans factory, others from Chino where men such as Joe Sailer, later the Mayor of Oxnard, learned the mechanics of sugar beet processing. A large group consisted of the machine operators and sugar beet boilers. These skilled workers from Scandinavia, France, and Germany found the wide-open spaces and opportunities of Ventura County much more to their liking than the congested cities of the East. The Oxnard plant became a profitable source of employment for many of these men for the rest of their lives.

The conversion of much of the Oxnard Plain to sugar beets caused the Hueneme port to lose its main source of income. The lima bean and barley crops were greatly reduced. More significant to the demise of Hueneme was the coming of the railroad. The Southern Pacific spur from Montalvo across the new bridge to Oxnard caused the county's agriculture to be shipped directly to either San Francisco or Los Angeles. In 1901, Thomas R. Bard faced the unpleasant fact that for him and Hueneme, there could be no turning back. The Wharf Company was sold in 1906 for $40,000, less than one-third of the asking price.

Hueneme merchants, including Achille, saw the future well before Bard and the Wharf Company were willing to admit defeat by the railroad. On February 3, 1898, the following notice appeared in the *Hueneme Herald:*

> *"To whom it may concern, the partnership of Wolff and Lehmann, doing business in the town of Hueneme, is dissolved."*

Shortly thereafter, this notice appeared in the *Hueneme Herald:*

> *"Lehmann and Waterman, formerly of Hueneme have opened their new store on 5th Street in Oxnard."*

In this same month, water pipes were placed beneath the ground and cement sidewalks laid in the town of Oxnard, indications of Oxnard's future.

Local newspaper accounts assumed a forlorn and tragic tone. On September 20, 1900, hope had become wishful thinking, as reported in the *Hueneme Herald:*

55

Two views of brick bank building

"Our lively sister Oxnard has been most unkind to us in the past week by taking some of our good citizens for her own, but just wait until we get our promised big rain, we'll have the lead and a few of Oxnard's citizens to equal the matter."

However, even when the rains came, citizens continued to leave Hueneme.

Achille was one of those Hueneme residents who planned to live in the old seaside village while commuting to the job-rich new town. Historians of Oxnard during its early years agreed that Bank of A. Levy was among the first businesses, and only bank, to establish in the sugar city prior to 1900. Achille remained a resident of Hueneme for 12 more years after setting up business in Oxnard.

Farmers' wagons, Oxnard Plain

The first office of Bank of A. Levy, located in Oxnard, was a simple structure. Recorded comments about Achille's place of business are conflicting. It seems that in the first months the bank operated out of a wooden shack on Fifth Street. Upon completion of the Wolff and Waterman department store in 1898, Achille moved his safe and business to a corner of that store.

While these surroundings were more suitable for a financial institution than a wooden shack, Achille needed his own separate place of business. In early 1899, Achille purchased from Ed Albplanalp the first residence built in Oxnard. He had this building moved to a lot on Fifth Street and opened his first office. For 14 years, Achille commuted from Hueneme to Oxnard weekly. More than once he told his Hueneme friends that he planned to move to Oxnard "within a few years." He only did so after his children had grown up in the quiet community by the sea.

Achille's family was always first in his thoughts. In April of 1900, the Levys embarked on a long trip to Europe. They visited the Paris Exposition and renewed family ties in both Paris and Alsace. Before leaving, Achille drew up his will. Forty-six at the time, and in good health, the will reflected his concern for his family's security should anything happen to him while abroad. Henry Levy and Leon Lehmann were named executors should any reason prevent Lucy from acting as executrix of the estate. With four children involved, the property was divided into 16 parts to be transferred to the heirs as they reached certain ages. The daughters received equal shares with the son. Achille's mother, Francoise, who was also bequeathed a substantial amount, died in advance of his arriving at Mommenheim to visit her.

When the Levy family returned from Europe in 1901, Hueneme and Oxnard had undergone dramatic changes. Hueneme's population had diminished, and business at the wharf had faded dramatically. Oxnard, while still a frontier town, was no longer a tent city. Growth in this year was exemplified by the Third Street school house, built on land donated by the

Oxnard, circa 1900

A. Levy behind teller cage

Colonia Improvement Company. The school was a two-story building, with a basement. Growth was so rapid that before long, there were four classes being held in the basement.

Other buildings, two stories and built of brick, contributed to Oxnard's new skyline. North Fifth Street, between B and C streets, was the first to be lined with substantial structures. Two newspaper offices (the *Sun* and *Press Courier*), B. S. Virden's and I. M. Poggi's drug stores, a post office, three churches, and the Masonic Temple were several of the main buildings built while Achille was away. The new construction, featuring cement sidewalks, and water pipes, was impressive.

Most interesting to Achille was the new building erected on North Fifth and B streets. It was the Bank of Oxnard, advertising itself as the "Sugar Beet Bank." Henry Oxnard was founder and J. A. Driffill, Charles Donlon, and Jacob Mauhardt were on the Board of Directors. Achille faced a future of stiff banking competition. *(Oxnard Press Courier,* January 20, 1900). In the following years, he would prove more than equal to this challenge.

Within weeks of his return to Oxnard, Achille purchased the lot situated on the northeast corner of Fifth and B streets, across the street and a half block south of the "Sugar Beet Bank." When his bank was completed in May of 1902, Achille's promise of a truly magnificent structure for Oxnard was fulfilled. No expense had been spared on construction or decoration, with over-sized windows, ornate arches, and columned exterior window sills. Three different types of brick as well as marble were used. The windows let in plenty of light, illuminating the carved wood and brass interior.

Achille's opening of his first office in Oxnard did not mean that his base of operations in Hueneme was ignored. He spent less time there from this point on, leaving his bookkeeper in charge. Alpha Adams took care of business in Hueneme from late 1899 through September 1902, at which time he moved to Oxnard to take over as cashier of the new office. The advertisement for both establishments read:

Banking and Commission
A. Levy
Foreign Exchange in All Parts of Europe
Oxnard and Hueneme

After 1901, the volume of business in Oxnard greatly outdistanced Hueneme.

In these years, many Oxnard residents felt certain that they had been truly blessed. Nature's bounty seemed limitless. Weather was excellent, and crops flourished. Water sprang forth from artesian wells. A prominent well-digger of the era guaranteed to sink a producing well anywhere in Oxnard for $100 (*Oxnard Press Courier*, February 28, 1903). The night brightened, as the Sugar Beet Company subsidized the installation of electric lamps in both the downtown area and some nearby residential tracts. Another electric wonder was the railroad from Oxnard to Hueneme. It carried freight as well as passengers to the wharf. To protect the town, a modern fire department was built on B Street.

In 1903, there were 40 subscribers, Achille included, to the telephone exchange. New businesses established since 1901 included a lumber yard, a tennis store, three blacksmith shops, a harness shop, a bicycle shop, numerous restaurants, hotels, and a cigar store.

Business prospered for Achille. Between 1902 and 1905, the assets of the bank grew substantially. Achille remained a respected banker, enjoying his well-earned reputation as an astute businessman and concerned member of the Oxnard community. The financial community had served the interests of the growing town, resulting in the establishment of many successful business and agricultural concerns.

On July 20, 1905, years of effort culminated in the formal establishment of Bank of A. Levy. The *Ventura County Democrat* reported that 49 individuals had taken stock in Bank of A. Levy, with the initial capitalization of $200,000 required by state law. Achille's brokerage-bank became an incorporated banking institution. The officers at the time of incorporation were: A. Levy, President; Charles Donlon, Vice President; Alpha Adams, Cashier; and Henry Levy, Secretary. They were also directors, as were Adolfo Camarillo, Herman Hellman (a Los Angeles banker), Louis Maulhardt, James Leonard, and William Waterman, husband of Achille's daughter, Anna (*Hueneme News*, June 22, 1906). Of the $200,000 minimum required for legal capitalization, $108,800 was invested by Lucy and Achille. Other family shareholders were Henry Levy ($24,000 for 240 shares) and William Waterman ($4,000 for 40 shares).

A. Levy in his 60s

The family investment totaled $136,800, leaving $63,200 provided by other sources. The new corporation had no trouble finding the remaining investors.

Within a month of incorporation, Bank of A. Levy received a spate of publicity from an unexpected source. The local newspapers proclaimed that Achille be congratulated for his help in capturing a clever thief whose specialty seemed to be that of "raising checks." The ever watchful Achille noticed that a check for $200 had been altered, or "raised," from $5. The headline which described the episode read: "Oxnard Financier Corners a Crook." Local citizens were assured that their deposits were safe in Achille's hands. Coincidentally, not a single instance of bank fraud or robbery of any sort is on record for this era. Hueneme and Oxnard were, of course, small towns with few roads in and out. Strangers were noticed, and escape from an act of theft would have been difficult.

Further appreciation for the small size of the community and the concern its citizens shared was brought to light when the city of Oxnard began to debate the question of its incorporation. With two banks now operating within Oxnard, a concern arose as to where to place city deposits, Bank of A. Levy or Bank of Oxnard. The conflict was resolved when Leon Lehmann, a candidate for the office of City Treasurer, stated that, if elected, he would divide city deposits equally between the two banks. This decided, Lehmann was then elected Treasurer. In 1903, Oxnard became an incorporated town, and its financial loyalties were split between Achille and the Oxnards.

Achille's clientele began to change after 1905. The booming mercantile community of Oxnard looked to the bank for support. Achille's interaction with the communities of Hueneme and Oxnard had been constant throughout his banking career. An example of Achille's community involvement is his loan of funds to begin the Baltimore Grotto, later known as the Oyster Loaf Cafe. Founded by John Cooluris in 1906, this restaurant soon established a reputation for being "the only place to eat in town." Achille dined there regularly. Cooluris looked to Achille for the capital necessary to be a restaurant entrepreneur. In partnership with his brother Pete, business flourished.

Many people suffered hard times from 1907 to 1913. The banking industry in the western states was hard hit. The source of these difficulties began with what has become known as the "Panic" of 1907. A flood of bank withdrawals began when investors came to believe that several important New York trust companies had over-extended themselves on loans. The rash of withdrawals soon spread to other Wall Street sectors. Soon, speculators of all sorts found themselves unable to borrow money to meet their financial obligations. During this emergency, President Theodore Roosevelt authorized large amounts of government cash to be put on deposit in New York banks. He also allowed U.S. Steel to acquire certain smaller steel companies when bankers told him the purchases were necessary to prevent the Panic's spread.

These measures only partially solved the problem. Money in circulation was too heavily concentrated on Wall Street and the East Coast. It could not be speedily transported in times of stress into areas that were most in need of ready cash, specifically, western banks. Thousands of small businesses went bankrupt, and farmers lost their farms to the banks.

Joe Levy

The Panic of 1907 continued to claim victims. The situation did not improve until 1913 when Congress finally put through the Federal Reserve Act. This legislation divided the nation into 12 banking districts, each under the supervision of a Federal Reserve Bank. Thereafter, the volume of currency for lending was controlled by a central directorship which adjusted interest rates according to inflation. It also provided cash reserves to certain areas when necessary.

The latter measure proved of lasting value but provided no help to Ventura County businessmen and farmers in 1907. The Collins and Sons Bank of Ventura was the only bank in the county to fail, as the elderly Collins was so unnerved by customers withdrawing funds that he shut down his operation the same year.

Local bankers, apparently at the instigation of Achille, proceeded to try ingenious schemes to carry their customers and themselves through the crisis. They organized into an association and, in lieu of money, issued scrip. This required a substantial amount of trust between banker and patron. The scrip and other short-term solutions worked, and soon the local bank runs stopped. Once again, fears were allayed by the forthright and far-sighted actions of the business community.

The hard times faced by Ventura County, as well as the rest of the nation, prior to World War I contributed to a so called "Populist" solution to economic ills. A united effort was begun by local farmers to form a bean growers union. On May 6, 1906, farmers formed the Ventura Lima Bean Growers Association, with the intent of more directly controlling the distribution of their crop. Interestingly, the growers engaged, as the manager of the Association, Julius M. Waterman, a grain broker who was also the brother of William Waterman, Anna Levy's husband. The farmers' new bean marketing organization also named Adolfo Camarillo as its Vice President. During the period from 1910 to 1920, the recovering economy and war years provided an ever-increasing market for beans. Waterman realized this and did not try to push the beans beyond their pre-Association price-setting standards. As a result of this, everyone prospered.

During the tumultuous years from 1904 to 1912, Achille and his family continued to reside in and enjoy the quiet life of Hueneme. There were rumors from time to time that he planned to erect a large residence in Oxnard and move the Levys there. This never happened, even though his youngest children were away much of the time, attending preparatory schools in Los Angeles. After 1906, son Joe was off to college at Stanford University where he remained most of the year. The oldest daughter, Anna, had been married in 1902, Julia in 1911, and Palmyre in 1912. Achille and Lucy stayed on in Hueneme. They enjoyed the company of old friends and familiar surroundings.

While the Levys enjoyed the atmosphere of Hueneme, they were also among its most progressive civic leaders. Examples of Lucy Levy's community involvement abound. In 1910, a minor conflict had arisen between Hueneme's two "horseless carriage" owners, Senator Thomas Bard and Charles Donlon, and the owners of stray cows and horses which wandered at will through the unpaved street, creating problems. The newly formed Hueneme Club took up the cause of the horseless carriages. The club, comprised of Mmes. Bard, Donlon and Levy saw to it that the constable enforced their wishes. Stray animals were then kept off the streets. The Hueneme Improvement Club's activities helped to modernize the town with numerous projects. In 1911, a library was begun, trees were planted along the main streets, and sidewalks were repaired. Lucy was active in all of these endeavors.

During these years, Achille performed many civic duties in Oxnard. In 1907, Achille helped finance the interior furnishings as well as the furnace for the Carnegie Library at Fifth and C streets. This neoclassic structure with its columns and ornamentation of

white marble, red brick, and tile was the gift of the
Scottish immigrant steel magnate Andrew Carnegie.
Oxnard was one of a number of towns nationwide
chosen for his generosity. The beautiful building
enhanced the rather bare town plaza center while its
contents enriched the minds of visitors. Long after
Achille's death, the Carnegie Library and Bank of
A. Levy buildings were still the two most outstanding
architectural structures in the downtown area.

Of interest during the years before World War I
is Achille's personal investment activity. During this
era, stock was an important part of the investment
portfolio of many people. For some, it was a hobby.
For many, it was a vocation and contributed significantly to their income. In the decade before World
War I, the market was frequently bearish. More than
a few Ventura County farmers who sought profit in
the stock exchange lost a substantial amount of money.

Achille recognized the uncertainty of where Wall
Street was heading. To him, the stock market was a
form of entertainment. The Southern Investment
Company, one of his first stock interests, sold in 1888
for 10 cents per share upon a capital stock of $100.
Between then and 1895, Achille acquired 1,465 shares
of Southern Investment Company stock at $10 per
share for a total investment of $14,650. This company
was the creation of Bard and was dependent on the
future of Hueneme's city and wharf. M. L. Wolff and
the Gerberding brothers were also prime investors. By
mid-July of 1895, the gamble was lost. Bard's venture,
which depended so heavily on increased wharf and
port commerce in Hueneme was clearly not the future.
The railroad had assured this. Achille still did not
abandon the Southern Investment Company. As a
show of confidence, he acquired yet another 1,655
shares at the new price of 10 cents a share. In the
following years, the value of the Southern Investment
Company was further reduced, with Achille losing his
investment.

In the years following, some of Achille's personal
investments took on a more esoteric nature. Between
1903 and 1912, he invested at least $3,500 in gold

Lucy Levy reading

mining stocks, perhaps at the suggestion of Scott Saviers. Saviers was an inventive and innovative spirit whose development of the mechanized lima bean planter had gained Achille's personal gratitude. It allowed Saviers to indulge in his dream of striking it rich in gold exploration. Achille's interest in the Oxnard-El Dorado Mining Company, the Bonnie Gold Mining and Milling Company (later known as the Star of the West), and the Junta Consolidated Gold Mining Company diverted a small amount of Achille's funds and much of his curiosity.

By 1912, both the family and professional situation of Achille had significantly changed. His son, Joe, had graduated from Stanford and returned to Oxnard to work at the bank. No longer was there a household in Hueneme, as Joe preferred to live in Oxnard. The new town offered more of a social life to a young man of 21. On weekends, Oxnard's young people congregated at the plaza area downtown featuring a pagoda and bandstand. Joe enjoyed the city's new tennis courts, a very popular spot.

For both Achille and Joe, the time was right for a family move. The Levys chose a double lot on the southwest corner of Second and D streets, surrounded on all sides by properties either already, or soon to be, occupied by relatives and old friends. The houses were of wood and two stories tall, featuring large sun porches. The yards were large and soon displayed extensive landscaping.

Bank of A. Levy continued to grow and prosper, a direct result of Achille's business acumen and personal banking philosophy. Capital surplus and undivided profits, those elements of banking which gave security to depositors and funding for local loans, rose from $340,000 in 1909 to over $500,000 in 1916, to $700,000 before Achille's death in 1922. One reason for this success is that the bank displayed steady growth in its commercial loan activity. Except for 1918, when war loans artificially bolstered the total loan amounts, Bank of A. Levy followed through on the conservative lending policies it advertised. Total resources almost tripled between 1909 and 1922, an indicator of good management and solid expansion.

In addition, the bank continued to demonstrate its commitment to the people and communities it served. Perhaps most impressively, the savings totals increased twelvefold from $73,000 to $883,000 during this span. Each year showed a substantial increase in confidence and investment of Ventura County residents in Achille's bank. The bank's "Report of Condition," in March of 1922, shows a slight downturn in savings and total resources, a reaction to Achille's death the previous month. By December of 1922, however, the total savings had jumped an unprecedented amount. Total resources reached new heights. This affirmation of customer confidence in Joe Levy's ability to run the bank was justified.

Achille was inventive and very active throughout his life. In the final year of his life, he still rigorously sought new fields of endeavor. The most significant of these projects was the Oxnard Building and Loan Association, founded on July 14, 1921. A. Levy was the new institution's first president, and the title was not an honorary one. *(Oxnard Press Courier,* June 29, 1963). Achille looked ahead to the future in 1921 as much as in 1885. He recognized that a lending institution could be fueled by the housing industry just beginning in Ventura County. Higher interest payments available to investors might threaten the savings account totals of his bank, but he was not about to let the new savings and loan business bandwagon pass him by. His early interest was a blend of both the conservative and innovative Achille Levy, demonstrating his ability to adjust to and capitalize on economic change.

Many remember Achille's later years. Recollections from the early 1920s differ little from written accounts of him from 40 years earlier.

> *"He'd always [be there] and was friendly and wanted to know how everything was and was like an 'uncle' to our family ... he was always such a cordial, friendly person and it was a pleasure going to the bank."* [15]

Available at the bank, Achille was also a visible personality on the streets of Oxnard. A number of people recall his "husky, but not stout" figure making the rounds of the business district and twirling a straight cane, much in the style of a European gentleman. The children of Oxnard were very happy to see his familiar figure coming down the street, knowing that the little leather pouch he always carried contained chips of chocolate. He gave out these treats after they had the chance to share their "news of the day."

These walks about town served Achille's purpose. They gave him the opportunity to check up on Oxnard businessmen and farmers he worked with, and they provided exercise. Most important, it gave Achille the chance to visit with the children of Oxnard, whom he dearly loved.

Achille never forgot his old customers and enjoyed visiting them in their homes. A poignant example of this practice were his visits to Loretta Maulhardt, the widow of his old friend and associate, Jacob Maulhardt. During her last illness, in the hopes that it might make her feel better, he visited often, bringing her a small carafe of brandy.

His interest in the crops and land never waned. For decades, Achille had traveled about the area in a buggy, sometimes with Adolfo Camarillo and others. He carefully surveyed the fields and visited with the growers. Toward the end of his life, his son-in-law, Jack Milligan, took him on his rounds in a horseless carriage. While much more ground was covered, Achille often complained to Jack, a dealer in horseless carriages, that the new vehicle's speed did not allow him to carefully inspect the crops.

With her children grown and the freedom to take part in community activities, Achille's wife, Lucy became much more active. Whether the subject was community affairs or recipes for "some of the most delicious cookies you'd ever want to eat," Lucy was known as an open and warm personality.[16]

Lucy's activities extended beyond the confines of her adopted city. In the period immediately following World War I, many veterans returned to Ventura County with little more than their uniforms. There were no pensions, no low-interest loans on housing, no educational assistance, and very little government support for injured soldiers. The Red Cross and its Ventura County affiliates were the only hospices available to these men. Auxiliaries were founded in Ventura, Santa Paula, Fillmore, and Oxnard. Lucy was on the County Board of Directors of the Red Cross and their efforts were invaluable. From 1918 through 1923, the year after Achille's death, Lucy participated in determining how these veterans might best be served. In these endeavors, she was assisted by her daughter Julia (Mrs. Jack Milligan). The volunteer work of Lucy, Julia, and Edith Hoffman, among others, was instrumental in helping veterans adjust to their post-war life.

Julia Levy Milligan

Lucy had other interests which held her attention well before Achille's passing. She enjoyed an independent financial involvement with a local pioneer family. Tom Vujovich, the member-manager of the Duck Club in which Joe Levy was the last surviving charter member, recalls that as a young Yugoslavian immigrant, his father, Mike, was loaned enough capital by Lucy to buy property northwest of Oxnard in 1918. Mike Vujovich did well with his 400 acres of walnuts, sugar beets, and limas, as did a number of other fortunate recipients of Lucy's personal loans. Many examples exist to show Lucy's concern for the immigrant European population who had a large part in the development of Ventura County.

While active to the end, Achille's health failed on

February 19, 1922. He went to bed with what his family thought was the flu. The next day, his color turned and his long-time friend and family physician, Dr. William R. Livingston, summoned his eldest daughter, Anna, from Los Angeles. She brought a heart specialist, Dr. Dudley Fulton. They arrived that afternoon, but it was too late to change the course of his illness. Achille died on February 20, 1922, at the age of 68. The official cause of his death was a dilation of the heart.

Jewish funeral services were conducted two days later in accordance with his faith, and with the participation of the Oxnard Masonic Lodge at Ivy Lawn Memorial Cemetery in Montalvo. The floral tributes paid to "Uncle" Achille by his friends were plentiful and colorful. His funeral procession was one of the longest in the county's history, forming a solid line of carriages and cars from the cemetery to downtown Oxnard. Thousands of residents from both sides of the river shared their grief in his passing.

Achille's business sense, ambition, and energy were a great boon to Ventura County. For four decades, the people recognized and acknowledged his contributions. While other people of Achille's status faced the classic distrust that farmers reserved for businessmen, Achille personally dealt with his share of anti-Semitism. Among his many attributes was his ability to encourage people to regard him as an individual rather than as a representative of these stereotypes.

A. Levy on hammock and A. Levy portrait

Chapter III

The Torch Burns On

Within days of Achille's passing, his son, Joseph, 36, was elected President of the bank by its directors. "J. P." was well known, having spent most of his life in Ventura County. Quotes in the local newspaper about Joe were reprinted by news agencies in Ventura, Santa Barbara, and Los Angeles. It was generally believed that his close association with his father had prepared him for his new position. However, despite Joseph's increased involvement with the bank, he had to prove his willingness to work for the county's best interests. The editor of the *Oxnard Press Courier* stated:

"He has only now to hew the line and follow the footsteps of his father and success for himself and Bank of A. Levy will follow."[17]

Information about Joe's childhood is in a memoir written by his nephew, A. A. Milligan, in 1982: "Joe was given to great fantasizing as a child, and used his imagination to the limit in teasing and tormenting his [three] sisters." While he was a great "tease" throughout his entire life, this habit was said to have been inspired by a desire to offer constructive criticism without being direct.

In 1906, Joe left Ventura County to attend Stanford University. Arriving just after the San Francisco earthquake, his interest in architecture and engineering was stimulated by the rebuilding of the city. During summers in Hueneme, his interest for planning was encouraged by engineer Roscoe Burson, who included Joe in the creative design and organization of the Ventura County Game Preserve Association. This 1,200-acre project near Point Mugu was Joe's hobby for the rest of his life.

Joe's determination to become Burson's apprentice engineer was staunchly opposed by Achille, who insisted that Joe be a banker. In his final years of college, Joe moved away from his engineering major. He received his Bachelor's degree in political science rather than economics. Undoubtedly, Joe followed his own ideas, independent and distinct from his father's.

Joe Levy

Joe's friendships at Stanford, especially those with "Doc" Avery (later a medical doctor) and Fred McCartney endured a lifetime. These and other Stanford alumni from Los Angeles often visited Joe. As parties and outings were only an occasional feature of Joe's youth, his collegiate camaraderie remained a precious memory to him. This strong bond with old friends was later to be enjoyed among the fraternity at the Ventura County Game Preserve, or "duck club."

Joe had a keen sense of humor even in the face of adversity. He also had a strong appreciation for little things. Joe is said to have had a wonderful personality and to have been thoughtful and kind.

Many of Joe's acquaintances of the early years recall his dress, described as "very neat," quite natty, but "nothing overboard." His attention to dress was restricted to six days a week throughout Joe's life, as on Sundays he would don the clothing of a farmer and head for the fields of Ventura County.

After Joe graduated from Stanford in 1911, and after his father convinced him that his future lay in banking, he moved into the Bank of A. Levy building on Fifth and B streets in Oxnard. During this time, he learned banking from the ground up, even serving a stint as janitor while also working full-time as a clerk and teller. Achille was a hard taskmaster, and a good teacher of finance.

Joe shared America's love affair with the automobile. One afternoon in 1911, this fascination for the speed offered by his new Maxwell touring car nearly cost him his life. He dislocated his shoulder and severed the motor nerve in his left eye, resulting in his eye being permanently turned inward. However, Joe's accident apparently did not affect his social or professional self-confidence. Those associated with him soon forgot about the entire matter.

At the bank, Joe continued to train under his father. The influence Joe exerted over his father is evident in the 1914 remodeling of the bank. Joe's knowledge of architecture was employed by Achille, and the reconstruction project included a number of Joe's ideas.

During this period, Joe's participation in the management of Achille's properties in Ventura County steadily increased. He became known for his successful management of Matilija Hot Springs, a well-known health spa near Ojai. The warm mineral baths were internationally acclaimed for their medicinal qualities, and attracted guests from all over the United States and Europe. The previous owners had let the spa and business fall into disrepair. In 1918, Achille took over the mortgage and gave Joe the job of restructuring the business. His son's success in the economic resurrection of Matilija left no doubt in Achille's mind that Joe was capable of a sustained and original approach to fiscal management.

A focal point in Joe's life was the Ventura County Game Preserve, founded in 1908. He had been responsible for much of its planning and development as an environment for birds, including mallards, sprig, teal, and widgeons. His talents as an architect and engineer were given full expression here, resulting in 1,200 acres of beautiful waterfowl habitat. Achille seldom visited, leaving Joe to run the entire operation.

From his mid 20s until his death, Joe devoted his mornings to hunting, enjoying scenery in the company of his friends. Joe enjoyed an enduring and profound happiness with nature and old friends. This bit of rustic life was a welcome refuge from an increasingly urban life.

Another of Joe's early enterprises was a farming development project near Los Mochis, known as the Quimichas Colony. It was undeveloped land quite isolated from anything resembling civilization. Although Achille appreciated its water and the potential of its farmland enough to become an original stockholder, he had little desire to venture into Mexico. Joe volunteered to act as his father's agent.

In 1921, he and other investors spent several weeks in and around Quimichas, camping out and hunting. Quimichas Colony passed their initial inspection, grew, and continued to prosper. However, Joe never returned to Mexico or even took an extended vacation ever again. After his father's death in February of 1922, his responsibilities in Ventura County allowed for few outside interests.

Upon Achille's death, many residents wondered

about the future of Bank of A. Levy. Although Joe had worked as clerk, teller, and secretary at the bank for 10 years, he had kept a low profile. It had been his father's business, and Achille had been active in bank and community affairs until his death. Remaining in the background, few knew much about Joe's qualifications. When clients read in the bank's advertisements that claims were attested to by J. P. Levy, Secretary, many were unaware of Joe's financial qualifications.

Joe Levy (left) with friends

Joe's early reputation fell just short of ideal. He set a pattern of coming in early (if it wasn't duck season), taking care of business such as checking loan applications, and then leaving until the afternoon. His secretary informed customers that Joe was out on banking business. In the mid-afternoon, Joe reappeared. He gave dictation and handled interviews and appointments. Many of his customers, especially those arriving in the morning, didn't know that Joe usually spent the late afternoon and much of the evening at his roll-top desk. Joe's desk's mountainous pile of material, as well as his unorthodox "filing system," became a legend during his tenure. His novel approach, in a profession so normally methodical and precise, reflected Joe's great powers of concentration and memory.

Joe's irregular business hours and social life raised eyebrows for a short while. These doubts were soon laid to rest, for Joe's raw intelligence and single-minded approach overcame the concerns anyone might have had regarding his abilities. His friendly attitude and thoughtful treatment of his customers and their families helped him gain the confidence of Achille's friends. Joe possessed the same precious ability to communicate that so distinguished Achille. His ability to relate to all types of people was vital to business success.

Times were changing, but the reception for customers at Bank of A. Levy remained constant through the tenure of Achille and Joe. Joe's availability to the customer was attested to by his first private secretary, Lucy Thiel:

> *"He just had a desk out there by the window [on Fifth Street] and I had a desk [next to Joe, with no partition] and that's all the privacy he had but he was always, when anybody came in, he was up there at the teller window with them, talking to them."* [18]

For three decades, Joe's open hospitality with bank customers was tempered by a cool and methodical approach to the management of bank funds. When people approached him for a loan, his standard procedures were rigorous:

> *"It wasn't easy to get money from Joe Levy. You went in there [to see him in person], you had to have a list made out of exactly what you were going to spend that money for. Right down to your grocery bill, your doctor bill, your light bill, everything had to be itemized. And that's what you had to spend that money for. And if you went in there [to Joe's office] to borrow $1,000, by the time you got out of there, he would convince you to get by with $500. And that is good training, you know."* [19]

Prospective borrowers had to be prepared for an onslaught of questions. Joe's study of prospective loan recipients included his own research of their financial history. Following his father's practice, Joe did his homework, methodically going through the cancelled checks of customers. He read the local newspapers with great interest, especially the "society" columns. Vacations, weddings, and gala parties cost a good deal of money. Joe kept a mental record of customers who overspent on these activities.

Joe continued to refine his approach to lending. Women's rights, starting with suffrage, had opened new vistas in finance. While Achille had given a farmer or merchant's wife consideration in the loan process, Joe took the equal rights mandate a step further. Independent career women and the wives of farmers and merchants were treated as equals and granted loans for various purposes.

Overall, Joe's lending policy was not that different from Achille's. It was personal and, by modern standards, perhaps primitive. But it was consistent, non-discriminatory, and, most importantly, it worked.

A critical factor in the bank's success was its employees. In 1922, three of the main officers had already worked under Achille at least a dozen years. Bob Durr began as a teller in 1909. He was third in tenure to Alpha Adams, who had been "borrowed" by Achille during the 1899 bean threshing season from Lehmann and Waterman. T. Russell Carroll began as a teller in 1907. Joe chose employees with the same care as his father. A strong source of help were local high school graduates. Each summer, the brightest were invited for interviews by Joe. The prospective employee's family background was carefully checked, generally back three generations. Joe always made it clear that he was looking for a person interested in a career, not for just a few months work. Durr, Adams, and Carroll stayed at the bank their entire working lives. Emerson Tucker and Ray Hanson, both hired by Joe in the early years of his presidency, also spent four decades at the bank. Joe's personal interest in his employees was genuine and went a long way in assuring their loyalty.

When Joe assumed the presidency in 1922, he was 35 years old and had worked under his father for 11 years. Though the community had endured its share of ups and downs, Bank of A. Levy had changed very little. Achille had created the bank's policies and Joe continued to implement them, while remaining responsive to the customers' needs. During these years, Joe's working hours, recreation, fiscal policy, and his life in general reflected his conservative outlook.

In the late 1920s and throughout the 1930s, Ventura County and the nation underwent extreme social and economic changes. Joe's steady business practices provided a sense of security for the community in an otherwise unpredictable world. He worked hard to see his customers through this difficult period, further gaining their trust and respect. He demonstrated his ability to adapt to change, a characteristic that would prove very important as Oxnard's population increased from 6,500 in the late 1930s to 25,000 by 1950.

During the mid 1920s, Oxnard's community feelings and optimistic outlook prevailed. On a wintry December evening in 1925, 1,500 people attended a dance and celebration of the sugar factory's past and future success. Joe Levy was there, as were most of Oxnard's leading citizens. Charles Donlon and John W. Rooney, the plant manager and successor to Mayor J. A. Driffill, had spared no effort in arranging the gala. Regrettably, Albert Maulhardt, the individual most responsible for the sugar beet industry coming to Oxnard, had passed away two years earlier. In his place were the rest of the Maulhardt family. Among those present were most of the "old timers" with whom Achille had made friends and done business. Times were prosperous, and everyone was quite anxious to have a good time. As Robert Maulhardt recalled:

"Old time dances as well as the latest steps, including the Charleston, were danced to the music of a six piece orchestra . . .

"The crowd entered into the festive spirit from the start and everybody had a most jolly time. The old square dances and the Spanish quadrille, which Ferd Roussey managed, were the hit of the evening among the old folks. At the same time there were enough of fox trots and one and three steps to please the younger set, who were there in large numbers.

"During the dancing, drinks were served at a regular old fashioned bar, foot rail and all. General employees of the factory were the dispersers of the thirst quenchers, which were nothing more than lemonade, both colored and au naturel."

These happy hours reflected the 10 excellent years of sugar beet production since the banner year of 1916, when one million bags of sugar were processed in the factory, and employees were given the bonus of an extra month's salary.

The town of Oxnard, and a substantial number of Ventura County residents, owed their prosperity to the sugar beet. However, events outside the local area, and outside the United States, caused a profound change in the market. As Joe Levy and his friends enjoyed their success at the sugar beet party, sugar beet prices had already begun to fall. Within a few years, there was such a glut on the world market that the factory nearly went bankrupt. As the evolution toward lower prices merged with the 1929 global business depression, Oxnard began to suffer.

Largely due to World War I, agricultural products from Oxnard and the rest of the United States brought high prices from 1914 to 1924. The devastation of its farmlands and economic disruption made Europe dependent on foreign goods. The sugar beet was one of the most important agricultural imports. Central Europe had thousands of acres of sugar beets put out of production by the war, a situation not rectified until 1921.

By 1924, European beet production had returned to its pre-war level. Due to the liberal loan policy of the United States government, millions of tax dollars were provided to European farmers. Much of this money went to growing beets. In Central Europe, the area devoted to growing beets increased 23 percent between 1921 and 1929, with dramatic results. After 1925, the prices dropped steadily worldwide. In 1923, for example, the price per pound was $2.80. By 1925, it had fallen to $1.60, and by 1932, $1.25 per pound. Several European countries protected their beet farmers with a high tariff on beet imports from the United States, their goal being economic self-sufficiency. By 1930, there was such a glut of beets that market prices fell drastically. United States producers were in big trouble.

From 1925 to 1930, American farmers produced more raw goods than could be consumed, leading to an adverse balance of payments. The United States' anti-Soviet policy, and the belief by business that the glut was temporary, encouraged the continuation of high production. Each year, prices for crops declined, and each year, the farmers planted as much as they could, assured that prices would rise the next season. This advice frequently came from bankers. The federal government's domestic policy was one of nonintervention in business, on the farm, or anywhere else.

The late 1920s were a period of mass euphoria for much of the industrialized world. Businessmen were making investments they would never have dreamed of several years earlier. The momentum of industry and production in the United States appeared to be only the beginning of good times for investors. Credit was easily obtained. Twelve percent interest on investments equivalent to over 20 percent today, was advertised as a risk-free average return. People invested widely and blindly, ignoring such monumental examples of economic disaster as the Florida land boom and following bust.

From 1922 through 1926, Joe worked hard to better accommodate the growing mercantile and farming community. During this period, he began to plan the construction of a modern banking facility to replace the original structure at Fifth and B streets. Joe made numerous sketches of the proposed bank. These were in the classical style and reflected the strong influence of architecture as taught at Stanford during Joe's tenure. The plans included an attached unit for Henry Levy, who had taken over control of Achille's agricultural brokerage business upon his death. Joe's concern and regard for his uncle are shown in the final plans for Henry's spacious office, which included a separate vault and lobby.

Modeled on the ideal of a Greek temple, the new building's rounded arches encompassed high windows with wide expanses of glass. The bank was an eye-pleasing edifice, allowing warmth and light to pass into the interior. The narrow yet elevated side windows with Doric columns between them, and the larger rounded arches of the entrance of Fifth Street called forth much the same balance between strength and beauty that characterized classic Greek architecture. Symbolizing dependability in the massive blocks of stone that soared 50 feet in height, it was an impressive structure.

The bank building in 1926

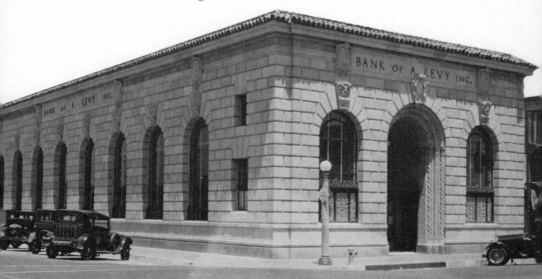

Interior of the 1902 bank building

Construction commenced in April of 1926. Joe had arranged for lumber, concrete, and marble to be transported to Oxnard on the railroad spur that then traveled along A Street. Over the next year, the progress of its construction became a spectator sport for many of Oxnard's 4,000 inhabitants.

Work was finally completed on May 23, 1927. The new bank structure fulfilled Joe's dream both for its architectural appearance and as a practical and pleasant working place for the bank staff.

The last few days before the open house were spent moving from the old building to the new headquarters. Young Arthur Achille Milligan, the then 9-year-old grandson of Achille Levy, recalls having seen deputies with sawed-off shotguns guarding the bank and transporting the money and safe deposit boxes.

The open house was a grand affair. Joe's staff had spent the previous month sending invitations to the Ventura County business community, and every banker and broker in the state and county with whom the bank had done business.

Interior of the bank, 1926

The old bank building was occupied by Poggi's Drug Store until 1942 when the Cooluris Brothers opened a liquor store and delicatessen on the premises. The upstairs rooms were rented out to a succession of professional people, including the legal practice of Irwin M. Lowe. After 50 years of service, the building was razed in 1963.

Lucy Levy was a most significant personal and professional link to both Achille and Joe. Joe never hesitated to admit to the profound influence that his mother had on his life. She was an influential and benevolent force in the lives of both men.

After Achille's death, Lucy increased her activity in the Ventura County Red Cross. Approaching 60, Lucy kept her chauffeur, Bert Kempster, quite busy driving her 1923 Cadillac around Ventura County. She devoted much of her time and energy to the Red Cross, serving on its Board of Directors from 1921 through 1925. Along with Julia Levy Milligan, Lucy was often actively involved in responding to some natural disaster. Emerson Tucker, who had just joined the bank during the mid 1920s remembers:

" ... many families in town were having financial difficulties and there were children going hungry, that food would be left on their doorstep for them and maybe some clothes ... she did a lot of this."[20]

Ruptured dam that caused flood

At no time was the Red Cross more vital than during the tragic aftermath of the Saint Francis Dam disaster on the morning of March 13, 1928. William Mulholland, who had gained a national reputation for designing dam projects, was given responsibility for the engineering of this dam above the town of Saugus. Mulholland built his huge structure on the basis of a faulty geological survey. Around midnight, the dam crumbled into the valley below, sending hundreds of acre-feet of water downstream. The devastation was awesome. The towns of Saugus, Piru, Fillmore, and Santa Paula were devastated by the slow but constantly moving water, mud, and debris. Hitting Fillmore at about 1 a.m., 385 people lost their lives. More than a thousand homes were destroyed or badly damaged. There was great damage to fields and orchards, and 7,900 acres of land were flooded. Flood waters even reached Oxnard.

Ravages of flood in Ventura County

Those who escaped the wall of water didn't realize the dimensions of the tragedy. Lucy Levy did.
One of the first local residents contacted by the Red
Cross, she acted decisively. Going from house to
house in her Oxnard neighborhood, she requisitioned
blankets and food for those displaced by the flood.

More damage caused by flood

Lucy took a special interest in the staff at Bank of A. Levy, assuming the role of "grandmother" to Joe's adopted family. Their 12-room residence often hosted bank staff, customers, and acquaintances.

Lucy had always been a concerned citizen. Her projects were carried out in a very private and low-profile fashion, and she always insisted that there be no publicity. Her humanitarian efforts against hunger and misfortune continued as long as she was physically able to move about.

In 1928 and 1929, farm prices continued their downward trend. An increasingly large portion of investors required ready cash to continue their financial activities. By October 24, 1929, such a number of them cashed in their stocks that others worried that the market was falling apart. In a panic, almost 13 million shares of stock were traded that day.

By Christmas of 1929, an entire era had ended. The next ten years would witness the Great Depression. Poverty would become a way of life for nearly 40 million people. Squalid villages called "Hoovervilles," named after the president whom many blamed for the Depression, sprang up in many cities.

Farmers everywhere, especially those living in areas heavily dependent on a single crop such as Oxnard, struggled to keep on their feet as crop prices dropped to new lows. Farm families in Oxnard had the resolve to ride out these tough years. They knew they could count on Joe Levy and his bank to help. He did just that.

Most bank customers learned of "Black Tuesday" in their newspapers or radios after the calamity had already occurred. The next day, when anxiety over the market's condition took hold, Joe Levy made instant personal loans to those who demanded cash. In doing so, he forestalled the general panic that destroyed so many smaller banks during the next two years.

From 1929 to 1931, much of Joe's time and money was devoted to ranching in the Somis area. Located at the end of Donlon Road, the Rancho Portezuela was purchased in the late 1920s by Joe, Dr. H. F. Rey, Robert Lefever, and Carl Grether, Sr. Oil deposits on the land had been a factor in the acquisition, however none were found. Joe played a large role in developing Portezuela into one of the first large lemon and walnut orchards in the area. Throughout the Depression, he spent many Sundays on this property, the Hamlin Ranch, and other properties in the Saticoy and Moorpark-Somis area. Joe trusted and respected the people who had patronized his bank after the stock market crash in 1929. In the following three years, he stuck to the conservative policies he had followed before the panic.

His family had substantial assets from the estate of Achille and holdings in ranch land throughout the county, as did numerous other banking families and corporations throughout the country. Loans were heavy and mortgages were still at the high prosperity levels. Many farmers came to Joe with their property deeds, unable to meet their obligations. Throughout the Depression, he refused to take their property.

During the decade of the Depression, the bank received assistance from its correspondent banks in order to maintain the necessary liquidity to meet the needs of its customers. These banks, Farmers and Merchants National Bank, Anglo California National Bank, and Bank of America, deposited cash in the form of certificates of deposit, for a specified number of days. Lack of liquidity at Bank of A. Levy was caused by Oxnard being an impounded agricultural community. When the Reconstruction Finance Corporation (RFC) was founded, the bank borrowed nearly $700,000 from it. No longer did the bank have to look to its correspondent banks for liquidity.

"Black Friday," as the bank holiday of March 6, 1933 came to be known, was President Franklin D. Roosevelt's first measure to stabilize the nation's currency. All the banks were closed until the RFC was operating.

Runs on banks were increasing. Several states declared bank holidays of their own, California included. In his inaugural address, Roosevelt set forth his program in bold terms, stating that he would ask Congress for a grant of executive power as potent as wartime powers. The president sought " . . . to wage war against an emergency as if we were in fact invaded by a foreign foe." His first action called for the federal government's strict supervision of banks, and an end of their speculation in common stock.

A number of banks closed as soon as they learned of the president's order. Others waited, among them Bank of A. Levy. Joe remarked that he took the forced closure as an insult. Nevertheless, a state banking official, who called Joe on the night of March 5, warned him that the official telegram of closure would arrive the next morning.

Tellers at the bank prepared for closing while Joe pondered the problem. A number of customers who had heard that banks would be closed on March 6 were already gathered in front. Although everyone knew the content of the telegram, Joe left the document unopened. Writing a personal check for several hundred dollars, he cashed it and authorized T. Russell Carroll, his cashier, to do the same with his own check. Carroll took his and Levy's cash and went out into the street. The telegram was opened and closing signs were posted on the front door. Carroll, out on the street amongst the gathered crowd, made personal interest free loans to friends of the bank in sums of $5 to $25, all on a verbal basis. Joe was able to forestall a panic. Joe's contemporaries agreed:

> *"Achille Levy would have liked this manner of business."*[21]

Within several days, the government allowed bankers to cash personal checks up to $25. In most banks, this service required a personal appointment with the manager. Joe gave his tellers approval to cash checks for anyone they knew and did not limit them to customers of Bank of A. Levy. Roosevelt's decree at once stimulated merchants to accept checks in lieu of cash.

The final innovation in Roosevelt's plan was his insistence upon deposit insurance. Many banks had made loans and other investments without regard for deposits in case of a bank's failure. Joe saw this federal role in protection of the depositor as a misguided attempt to revive banks that had squandered their clients' funds in bad investments. He believed that if a bank needed deposit insurance, it shouldn't be in business.

As these new guidelines made their way into banking, Joe decided to make an innovation of his own. While waiting for the RFC to examine the bank's books behind the legally locked front door, Joe left the side door of the building open to customers. This enabled them to get in and conduct bank business.

Until the bank was allowed to reopen, the "side-door" activity involved services and personal loans made by the Levy family, without using depositor funds. As the Depression deepened, more and more of the Levy's personal fortune went out in loans. Much of it was repaid quickly, some not at all. Joe had no regrets. After the bank's solvency was officially recognized by the RFC and normal banking hours resumed, the side door was still left open until 4 p.m., should any merchant or farmer require attention. The phrase "the side door is always open" became part of bank folklore.

"Side door" banking continued throughout 1933. The strain of the Great Depression continued. In 1934, with both the bank's and the family's liquidity stretched, Joe looked further afield. Fortunately, the federal government loaned the bank $250,000 to help farmers and businesses through the hardest year of the Depression. The hub of Oxnard's economy, the sugar beet factory, was saved from bankruptcy by Roosevelt's economic program. During the early 30s, its stock had dipped to an all time low of 20 cents per share. Only the RFC subsidy to sugar beet farmers, and the factory itself, staved off bankruptcy.

The next five years were very difficult for most Americans, both urban and rural. Ventura County's welfare applicants numbered in the thousands. Individuals would receive a monthly warrant issued by the Board of Supervisors and bring it to the bank. The bank had to wait two weeks for these warrants to be honored by the federal government. It is noteworthy that the system was seldom violated, and the bank always got its cash back from the government.

Many of those fortunate enough to retain their jobs either took a cut in pay or remained earning the same wages for the rest of the decade. Joe took a 10 percent cut in pay and his officers, tellers, and bookkeepers saw no increase until 1940.

The hardships this caused were recalled by former teller Ray Hanson. Hanson's neighbor was a highway patrolman and one day Hanson was informed by the officer that a dead seal was on Highway 101 just north of Ventura. An offer of $3.50 to properly bury the seal sent Hanson scurrying up the coast.

People from all over the country, especially the Midwest "Dust Bowl," came to California to pick up whatever jobs were available. These workers provided a reliable and productive labor force for this area's farmers and were happy to have work, lodging, and food.

In February of 1934, Lucy Levy died at the age of 71. From the bank's creation in the 1880s, Achille and Joe reflected the strength and sensitivity of the Levy family, with Lucy as the common thread. Coming from the cosmopolitan atmosphere of Paris to the rural environment of Hueneme, she made the adjustment to frontier life with both energy and grace. Her steadying influence upon the Levy men, taken in concert with her ongoing efforts for charitable and humanitarian causes, demonstrated Lucy's contribution to the welfare of her adopted country.

Now alone at nearly 50 years of age, Joe's personal activities changed after Lucy's passing. He became even more methodical and regular in his habits. He visited friends and relatives throughout the county frequently, enjoying their friendship. He worked hard at keeping the bank solvent and responsive to community needs.

Oxnard had a population of approximately 8,000 people during the 1930s and early 1940s. Joe was able to continue the practice of personal banking as had his father. He continued to meet with his patrons whenever a problem or opportunity arose, and knew each of them on a personal basis. Farmers still entered the bank in their work clothes and boots without an appointment and spent much of the afternoon with the bank president. Some referred to this periodic obligation to see "Uncle Joe" as their trip to the "sweat shop."

During the Depression, bank examiners made frequent visits to banks throughout the state. The arrival of these state bank examiners was a cause of great anxiety to many bankers, for they had the power to close a bank. Examiners calling at Bank of

Lucy Levy

A. Levy regularly warned Joe not be so trusting with his customers.

While the bank examiners enjoyed Joe's mealtime hospitality, no discussion of business took place. These dinners provided a forum in which he preached about the underlying economic wealth of the county. The next day, when they were down at the bank, he would discuss loan policies.

Joe's defiant stance against the bank examiners was made possible by knowledge gathered from many hard working hours. His meticulous attention to financial affairs required a devotion to detail that many people in Joe's position simply did not have. Joe worked until seven or eight o'clock every night, catching up on banking details after closing.

Joe regarded foreclosure not only as a client's failure but also as one of his own. When a disheartened individual approached Joe with talk of foreclosure, his immediate response to plans for selling off property to repay loans was adamant. To Joe, foreclosure meant a mutual failure of banker and patron, and he simply would not allow it. In both farming and business, Joe's approach was the same. Merchants, such as the owners of the Oyster Loaf Cafe and the Greek grocers across the street from the bank, recall his stalling off foreclosure many times. Often, loan patrons didn't even have the land to mortgage in order to prevent foreclosure. In this instance, the bank was offered a chattel mortgage for collateral. The bank once took a note on six mules named Whitney, Old Gray, Sally, Crazy Ida, Big Bill, and Little Jack. Often, however, these yearly payments didn't make a dent in their outstanding loan. Joe simply called them in at the end of the year to sign yet another note.

During the mid 1930s, Joe began to suffer from arthritis, and the disease became progressively worse over the next decade. His life became sedentary, as he was often racked with pain. Swollen ankles and knees kept him off his feet much of the time. His professional approach, however, did not reflect his personal anguish. His message was one of optimism.

Joe's concern for the welfare of others never slackened. As the Depression entered its last years and recovery began, Joe was always there with an encouraging word. This encouragement to the farmer and merchant was crucial to their eventual success.

With the end of the Depression Joe devoted more time to new interests. He had long enjoyed short trips to the Simi, San Fernando, Santa Rosa, and Conejo valleys for relaxation and sport. Joe's interest in the eastern valleys, however, was not limited to recreation. In Achille's time, the dry farming capacity of these hills and plains produced barley and lima beans. Joe's ambition was to expand the horizon of this section by planting orchard crops. Citrus, walnuts, and apricot trees began to sprout in the old lima bean and beet fields. The Levy-Camarillo ranch, known as Tierra Rejada, was devoted to apricots, and Joe managed it.

The potential of previously uncultivated acres also was appreciated by Joe and others. There was a gradual transition from lima bean operations into various different agricultural crops and housing. This was accomplished by Jake Smith, a Bank of A. Levy customer for 30 years. Smith had been involved with the Perkins Ranch, later to become Las Posas Estates near Camarillo, through Janss Investment Corporation (JIC). JIC was run by Dr. Edwin Janss and Harold Janss. They owned about 10,000 acres in Conejo Valley which is now the core of Thousand Oaks. JIC was a successful development and financial corporation, and the city of Westwood was a product of the Janss brothers' vision.

Constant experimentation in new crops and agricultural engineering were a feature of Eastern Ventura County until 1950, when residential development began. In this environment, Joe was in his element and easily forgot the pain from his arthritis. An additional motivation to buy into the valley area was that flat land was simply becoming too valuable to hold anything but crops.

The landscape changed, and much of this transformation in the East County could be directly or indirectly attributed to Joe Levy. Levy interests throughout the area were substantial. Bank of A. Levy was financially involved with many East County ranchers during the 1930s and '40s, especially in Somis, Moorpark, and Simi.

Joe had an extensive involvement in soil conservation. Topsoil, that crucial foot of earth containing essential minerals and decayed organic matter, renewed by regular plowing, was the common bond between all involved in agriculture. This thin ribbon of fertility meant the difference between farming for profit or simply for survival.

In 1940 and 1941, Joe made a most important decision. The partnership with farmers during the Depression had done much to bring his bank and local agriculture back to a strong position. The President of Bank of America, A. P. Giannini, sought sound investment possibilities and came to Oxnard looking to expand the holdings of the nation's largest financial institution. A member of the advisory board of Bank of America in Oxnard, Adolfo Camarillo was also an old friend and confidante of Giannini. At a board meeting at the local Bank of America branch was the following discussion:

> " . . . while discussing matters generally as they did at the end of the business part of the meeting, Mr. Giannini said to Adolfo Camarillo, 'We may be moving the bank before too long.' Adolfo said, 'Is that so?' He said, 'Yes, I have been talking to Joe Levy about buying Bank of A. Levy. And he is going to let me know after this meeting whether he wants to sell it. I think he will because I told him, when I asked what he wanted for it, he said, 'I don't know,

I don't know if its for sale even.' So I left him with this statement: You name the price that you'll sell for, just so long as its within reason, and I'll buy it.'"[22]

As told by Hap Maxwell, a local lawyer and farmer, Joe's response went:

"Well, with that big a leeway, one would imagine that Joe Levy would have built that price up to what he thought was the maximum Giannini would pay for it, but he didn't. He refused to sell. If he had, Bank of A. Levy would have stopped in its tracks. And that was before 1941. It showed the foresight of Joe Levy, because he not only maintained his responsibility for continuing the dynasty of his own family but Bank of A. Levy is worth a great deal more than Mr. Giannini would pay for it now. It bore out his view of the future."[23]

The bank remained a local institution. Perhaps Joe never even considered selling out. He loved to talk and draw people into discussions on their opinions and plans. His conversations with Bank of America may well have been without serious intent.

In 1940, Arthur Achille Milligan entered the equation for success at Bank of A. Levy. Called "Bud" by both family and bank staff, he was regarded as a special favorite by grandfather Achille from his birth in October of 1917. Bud was the third son of Achille's youngest daughter, Julia, and Jack Milligan. Grandfather Achille was pleased that this child was named for him and proclaimed Bud a "true banker" at birth. At the birth of each of his grandchildren, and on each Christmas and New Year's thereafter, Achille gave each a substantial monetary gift.

High school was not much of a challenge to Bud. A schoolmate recalls:

"It just never ceased to amaze me what a great student he was and what good grades he got and

*how little studying he did and he'd come home with
every exam, A,A,A, you know.''*[24]

A. Levy with young A. A. Milligan

After completion of high school, Bud followed
his Uncle Joe's path to Stanford University, majoring
in banking and business. He later stated: ''I can't
really pinpoint a time when I decided I would go into
the bank . . . it was more or less decided for me. I was
a product of family brainwashing.''[25] He enjoyed his
undergraduate days and studies at Stanford and continued on to graduate school in business from 1938
to 1939.

Bud was eager to see the world outside Oxnard,
and left Stanford in 1939 to visit Europe. The traveling Americans abroad were advised to return home,
and Bud traveled by freighter back to California, via
the Panama Canal. ''After I came back,'' Bud said, ''I
fiddled around for two or three months, then worked

100

Snapshots of A. Levy with young A. A. Milligan

A. A. Milligan as college student

briefly for the Department of Agriculture, doing a land usage study. Then I went where I knew I would wind up, in the bank."[26]

On April 28, 1940, he started at the bank as a trainee bookkeeper. Joe, to teach his nephew all aspects of the business, started Bud at the bottom. The Stanford graduate swept, mopped, and cleaned the bathrooms. For more than two years, Bud worked as a full-time bookkeeper and clerk. In 1942, on his 25th birthday, he went on active duty in the Navy. A month later, he married his college sweetheart, Jeanne Welch of Sacramento. They honeymooned at Ithaca, New York, where Bud was at the Cornell Navy Indoctrination School. He served until the end of the war, first doing eight months of shore duty in Panama, followed by two years as a gunnery officer and navigator on an Atlantic destroyer.

While the Navy sent many boys all over the world, they also sent groups of 10,000 men at a time to Port Hueneme for Seabee training. These men forever transformed the Hueneme-Oxnard scene. They and their families stimulated housing and shopping services well beyond what these rural communities had to offer. Bank of A. Levy staff made great efforts to serve the financial needs of these new Oxnard residents.

The effects of the war were especially unfortunate for the Japanese-American residents of the area. The Western Defense Command of the U.S. Army ordered more than one half of the "Nisei" population of Oxnard to the Gila River Relocation Center in Arizona. The safety deposit boxes of 400 Japanese-Americans were sealed by federal agents, denying them access to their own belongings.

The war continued on through the summer of 1945. As the Allied Forces gradually shifted from the Atlantic to the Pacific Theater, things got more hectic. Emerson Tucker recalled that the bank's function during these times was as a check cashing facility, having to trust total strangers. He felt that it was his patriotic

A. A. Milligan as a Navy officer, 1942

duty to provide the service and take the risk:

> *"I can't begin to tell you how many people came in
> to cash a check. Wives would come out [to Oxnard
> and Hueneme] to see their husbands, as this was
> the shipping point for all Seabees going out to the
> construction work on the islands. More were out
> here than in Los Angeles, believe it or not, in those
> four years so many wives would come here and
> have one farewell night with their husbands and
> never know where they were shipping out to . . .
> And that's the way it was. And unfortunately, little
> banks back in the Midwest, even big banks in the
> East would tell them, oh you can get a check cashed
> out in California. When you tried to cash a check in
> a foreign area where you weren't known, out of
> state, at some little bank that maybe was capitalized
> at $250,000 or $500,000, they couldn't take many
> chances and the other banks wouldn't. We took
> some risks, we cashed an awful lot of checks and
> only had one loss [an officer whose wife closed their
> account and moved]."* [27]

The war also had its effect on the status of women.

Previously, only men had been tellers. L. M. Spencer, a retired Assistant Vice President of the bank stated:

> "Women were stenos or did escrow work once in a while. World War II changed all that. As men were drafted into military service, women took over the jobs which had traditionally been held by men. But when the war ended, it was impossible to resume the old ways. As we went along, there were more and more women in the banks and my wife began to kid me about my harem."[28]

One such woman was Georgette Kane, whom Joe hired in 1944 as his secretary. She remained with the bank for 17 years. While her most significant professional contributions to the bank came after the war, Mrs. Kane remembers that one of her duties had been to supply Joe Levy with See's chocolates. As the nearest See's was in Los Angeles, she kept track of staffers traveling there so that they could make the purchases.

As the war continued and his arthritis grew worse, Joe's business and professional habits remained constant. He enjoyed helping out friends, often those of Achille or his old friends. In 1942, he financed and helped design a new house for the newlywed John Deboni. Joe became deeply involved with the details of the project. The Debonis spent three nights a week at Joe's house, working on the plans. Finally, after considerable review and modification, building began.

In April of 1945, the war in Europe ended, and in September, it ended in the Pacific as well. Bud returned to the bank as keeper of the general books and would, slowly, rise in influence. People saw Bud ride to work on his bicycle and knew he was the man who would guide Bank of A. Levy into the future. They also knew that he was a strong link with the past. A great many friends and customers saw much of Achille in young Bud and were happy that he was back.

Agricultural methods and crops began to change drastically around 1938, and events moved even faster after 1945. Irrigation replaced dry farming on an ever-increasing scale. The high real estate prices of the post-war land boom in the Los Angeles area also had a profound effect on Ventura County. Carrots, tomatoes, lettuce, and celery were vegetables that were established prior to 1950. After the war, farmers planted two to three vegetable crops on the same ground in the same year. Crop rotation became commonplace in local agriculture during the 1950s.

There was tremendous population growth. From 8,000 in 1940, Oxnard grew to 25,000 people in 1950. A primary cause for this increase was the Navy personnel and their relatives based in Port Hueneme and at Point Mugu. Many sailors who passed through Port Hueneme on their way to the Pacific decided to return to the region after the war. These men brought their families and put new and sometimes overwhelming demands on Oxnard's resources. In its first 75 years of existence, Bank of A. Levy had always been a relatively small bank servicing a largely agricultural area. These new immigrants required homes and services that the small farming community could not provide. They required banking services that Joe had not even considered before the war. Mercantile and industrial business saw in these new people a labor force which did not require the high wages paid in the Los Angeles area. Large banking chains recognized their great potential as investors and customers and were more than willing to provide these services. All these factors placed great strain on Joe and the bank.

A most striking change to Oxnard came with the closing of the sugar beet factory. The economic backbone of the community for over 50 years, the local industry was no longer able to compete with imported cane sugar from Hawaii and other sources. In addition, sugar was no longer being exported to Europe. The land upon which the Oxnard factory stood was more valuable for real estate and agriculture than for sugar. It was sold for $1,600 per acre, and the factory was razed.

One major feature of Oxnard life in post-war years that did not change significantly was Joe's bank. In 1950, it still operated on its original $200,000 capital, had a surplus of $400,000, undivided profits of $781,611 and deposits of $11,356,767. It stood out as a successful example of a well managed, privately owned bank in an era of financial institutions. The habits that Joe had acquired over a lifetime did not change with the new times. People enjoyed seeing Uncle Joe getting around, and he was well liked for his idiosyncratic behavior.

A middle-aged Joe Levy

In later years, Joe's activity was greatly restricted by his health. By 1950, he was barely able to walk, as getting up out of his chair was painful. This was especially disturbing to a man who had been athletic and active throughout his life. It curtailed duck hunting, his favorite recreation. Bud was a witness to Joe's illness and his courage:

> "It became progressively worse for 15 years until
> [1951] when he became a "guinea pig" as one
> of the first four or five people in the West to be
> treated with A.C.T.H., the forerunner of cortisone
> ... From a person wracked with pain, with swollen
> knuckles and knees, unable to wade a duck pond or
> be on his feet any length of time, all of which created
> a somewhat depressed man, he seemed relatively
> free of pain and an almost euphoric optimist, want-
> ing to get back where he was in 1912 when he
> wanted to re-engineer his world, building roads,
> digging water wells, planting orchards."[29]

This new youthfulness and positive outlook was only one face of a two-sided coin. As Bud remarked:

> "The A.C.T.H. had its side effects, and Joe never
> really did follow his doctor's orders as to diet. By
> 1954, he was getting to the bank anywhere from
> noon to two p.m. and not really able to drive him-
> self to any sustained effort. He was mentally very
> keen, he never lost that."[30]

Joe was still determined to run his bank exactly as he had for over 30 years. An appropriate example of his banking style were his roll top desks, the one in his office and another at home in his study. The youngest of Bud's boys, Marshall Milligan, recalls clearly:

> "When I was a small child ... I can remember
> going over to his house in the afternoons on Satur-
> day or Sunday and visiting him in his upstairs
> study. He would have me sit on his lap, open his
> roll top desk and show me the stuff in it."[31]

Joe knew where most, perhaps all, of the papers on his desk were. If no one else knew, it was just as well, as Joe insisted on taking a personal hand in any business transaction. If records, notes, or his signature were needed, all waited until he was there to personally find them or sign them. Joe had an excellent mind for details, and he knew it. For 25 years, he carried most of these facts around in his head. What wasn't there, he could eventually find in his desk.

Automation became a profound issue in the 1940s. The war had done a lot to develop and advance technology. The 1950s were even more dramatic in their emphasis on perfecting and expanding earlier technology, especially computer technology. Joe followed the technological revolution, but automation was not yet available or practical for the smaller bank. Well into the 1950s, his staff was still doing the same work by pre-war bookkeeping methods that larger banks quickly accomplished with a new generation of equipment.

Joe's reluctance to delegate authority and his insistence on doing everything himself presented a problem for Bud and the staff. Occasionally, the situation was also frustrating to those who did business with the bank. For the Deboni family, a business visit to the bank took most of the day. Bud would have to sit and wait patiently for Joe to finish working out minute details.

An important result of Joe's insistence on total control of bank affairs was that there were no branches of the bank established until after his death. When Bud proposed opening new branches early in the 1950s, Joe simply refused to consider it. Advertising under Joe's presidency was exactly the same as when his father ran the bank. Perhaps Joe's apparent lack of concern for attracting new bank patrons stemmed from his realization that they would have presented too great a strain on his personal resources and those of the bank. He felt comfortable dealing with farmers. For the most part, the new residents were in other businesses.

Those who had enjoyed a profitable relationship

with Bank of A. Levy from its inception to World War II were of special significance to Joe. He had known three generations of these families. He took it seriously when they called him "Uncle Joe." Many of the 8,000 people in pre-war Oxnard were members of Joe's "extended family." He liked that situation and did not want to give it up to accommodate the strangers moving into Oxnard.

On May 13, 1955, long-time employee Alpha Adams passed away. Mr. Adams had first worked at Achille's Hueneme office in 1899. He had moved to Oxnard in 1902 to take over as cashier at his new location, and had remained an officer of Bank of A. Levy from that time until his death. He was a permanent feature of the bank for over 50 years. To those who didn't know him well, he was stern and difficult to approach. Mr. Adams, who by 1950 was in his late 70s, was also well known for naps at his desk.

On July 20, 1955, the bank celebrated the 50th year of its incorporation. It was a gala occasion, and the last time "Uncle Joe" had the company of old friends, family and customers. Bud and Jeanne Milligan were on their vacation during this festive, day-long celebration, allowing Joe to enjoy the individual attention of all present. He continued to put in his hours at the bank through July of 1955, when his condition once again turned for the worse. As Dutch Linnett, a member of the Board of Directors recalled:

> *"You never heard him "belly aching" about it (his health), and it seems to me he put in his hours practically right up to the last days."*[32]

Uncle Joe's death on August 17, 1955 was not a surprise to his inner circle of family and friends. Joe's nephew Bud remembers his uncle's generosity and strength of character.

> *"Joe was generous. He never thought of himself first. He was not a churchgoer, but was truly reli-*

gious. He had been raised by the Golden Rule and Ten Commandments and he staunchly believed they were the only way to live. He tithed himself, making cash gifts every year to a substantial number of charitable and educational agencies. He made personal loans out of his own pocket to any number of people including staff of the bank, always at very reasonable interest and almost always without security. And his generosity extended into his appraisals of people. He never took advantage of his position or of another person's misfortune or lack of strength. He never asked anybody to do what he himself had not done when he was physically able to do it. He had the courage of his convictions, and was steadfast in supporting them."[33]

Joe felt an affinity for his Jewish heritage. Throughout his life, he and his mother, Lucy, were supportive of the plight of European Jews. As with Achille and Lucy, Joe was also concerned for the welfare of displaced Jewish orphans. While this interest in ethnic and family background was of great importance to Joe, it was but a part of his overall concern for people. Edward Kraus was for many years the Ventura County Chairman of United Jewish Appeal. He remembers Joe as a person who was devoted to the community and who was interested in civic affairs of all sorts. During banking hours, he would speak only of bank business; however, after hours, he was remembered as often discussing Jewish affairs. His Jewish heritage was of central importance to him. Joe looked to the Masonic Order, with its required observance of a god as "Supreme Being," for spiritual solace. He was President of the Masonic Association from 1952 until his death in 1955. It had been organized to plan and build a new temple.

As meticulous and well prepared as Joe normally was for any possible change in events, he did not draw his own will. This came as a surprise to his old friends, long accustomed to his practice of helping and advising others on their wills. Joe's interest in the welfare of others had taken precedence over his own personal affairs.

Joe Levy with J. B. Lapeyre, tenant of the Levy-Camarillo ranch, Tierra Rejada

Chapter IV

A New Horizon

The sense of loss at Joe's death was easier to bear with the knowledge that Bud Milligan was taking over the helm. Bud stood ready to guide the bank's expansion in an era of unprecedented growth and change.

For the next decade, the bank was at a crossroads. Bud's innovative nature would prove to be just what the bank required for the dizzying changes that took place in the '50s, '60s, and '70s. Bud proved to be the right man, in the right place, at the right time.

Bud's education, as well as his war service and early role in the bank have been described. His early and lifelong commitment to community affairs also deserves mention. Following the precedent of Lucy Levy's concern for returning soldiers requiring assistance after World War I, Bud showed concern for fellow servicemen and others in need after World War II. He led the Oxnard area Red Cross drive in 1946 and again in 1965. In 1947, he served as foreman of the Ventura County Grand Jury. In 1955, he returned to sit as a jury member. Other community service organizations that enjoyed his active involvement were the Boys Club of Oxnard (Director and President), Junior Chamber of Commerce, Oxnard Rotary Club, Ventura County Young Republicans, and the Community Chest.

During this period he and his wife, Jeanne, were also busy raising their two young sons, Mike and Marshall. Both were in grammar school when Bud took over the bank in 1955. From 1954 to 1956, his membership on the Oxnard High School Board required a good deal of Bud's efforts. One teacher at the time reported:

> "We had a big dispute with the Superintendent and there was a terrible uproar with the teachers and administration and poor Bud was in the middle of it being on the school board, but I remember him very gratefully at that time because he was extremely objective about the whole thing."[34]

Bud kept up a fast pace at the bank in early 1955. Earle Glenn was impressed:

> "I became a teller in February of 1955, and I can remember that none of us on the west side of the bank, when we worked on that side as tellers, none of us would ever leave our cage without looking both ways because Bud was a storm when he wanted to go from his office to the vault or coming back from the vault. He was always on the run. Lunch . . . and he'd be running out to his car"[35]

Bud also enjoyed horseback riding. The Rancheros Adolfo were a group of local ranchers and businessmen who, in 1950, began the tradition of three-day horseback rides as a warm-up for a larger state-wide social event that took place in Northern California. The local event was named after Adolfo Camarillo and included a dramatic play as part of the festivities. Participants remembered:

> "So they needed a throne and Bud was out riding his horse and they decided to use his brand new Cadillac front seat as the throne. [Most of us didn't] have the guts to pull it out of there because we all do business with him so Bob Duntley, who didn't let a little thing like Bank of A. Levy worry him, got in the Cadillac and took the whole damn thing apart, electric seat and everything. Bud Milligan came back and I thought he was going to have a stroke. I don't think he ever got that seat put back in right."[36]

Bud's dry sense of humor served him well. He took the car to Bob Nesen's (later the Ambassador to Australia) Cadillac agency to finish hooking up the electric seat, which was done at no charge. Bud had Dee Coker, the service manager, send Bob Duntley a phony repair bill for $300.

Bank of A. Levy customers could count on a personal interest from the President and staff. Madeline Meidema, one of Bud's teachers, was a bank patron since the 1930s. Her recollection of Bud's personality typifies him:

> "He's always been most kind to people. You know, he could forget you as far as that goes, but he'd always remember one's name and always has been willing to talk to you about your problems."

Personal contact with the customer was continually emphasized by Bud in his early statements.

> "There's only one thing you have to sell, the personal service of the people employed in the bank ... the products themselves are all the same: deposits, checking accounts, etc. The emphasis has to be on the people in the organization and dealing with those who are your customers."[37]

Achille, Joe and Bud always respected their clients and saw themselves in business to serve the needs of their customers.

During his first week as bank president, Bud received three different offers from larger banks to discuss selling Bank of A. Levy. Each was told "not to waste your time" pursuing the matter. This settled, Bud and staff were, he said, "busier than a one-armed paperhanger with a case of hives."

Advertising was an immediate concern. Within a few months of taking office, Bud improved the bank's visibility and defined its image more forcefully in

115

Fred Aggen (left), Bud Milligan (center) and Adolfo Camarillo

newspapers, radio, and outdoor media. Before Bud
became President, the small, simple sketch of the bank
building atop a few lines of print had served as the only
advertisement of Bank of A. Levy. This was replaced
by photographs, sketches, and printed messages.

The larger, state-wide banks presented a challenge
to Bud. Agriculturally rich and temperate, Ventura
County had lured an unprecedented number of new
people and businesses to the area as the 1950s pro-
gressed. Institutions such as Bank of America and
Security Pacific Bank were also established in the area.
They, as well as many other banks not previously doing
business in this county, appreciated the expanding
economy. Banking institutions proliferated in the
decade between 1955 and 1965. Bud commissioned
experts on banking expansion and market research
from Stanford Research Institute to do a study on the

A. A. "Bud" Milligan at his desk in the bank's Oxnard headquarters

bank's future in relation to projected growth. This study determined that if Bank of A. Levy did not expand, it would be unlikely to survive.

Plans for an office in Camarillo were underway from 1956 to 1959. After appropriate state and federal authorization procedures were met, land was bought. The site that was chosen as most promising for expansion was situated in downtown "Old Camarillo." Here the bank would be able to serve both the growing east and west segments of the county. The site was next to a wagon trail where ranchers from the East County had carried lima beans, barley, and other produce to Hueneme since the 1870s. Fisher and Wilde of Ventura were chosen as the architects, and during 1958 plans were approved and given to the builders, Treiberg and Ruesink of Ventura. The building was 5,300 square feet, built in a contemporary style with a beamed ceiling. A parking lot provided spaces for 28 cars and there was a drive-up window.

Tract homes in Ventura County, circa 1950

While the new building grew out of an old Camarillo bean field, Bud and his staff created the new personnel and accounting entities that formed the Camarillo operation. Delegating authority in an institution that prided itself on personal familiarity and service was a major undertaking. The customers who would patronize the Camarillo office had years of experience with Joe Levy, some even with Achille. Bud determined that familiar faces from the main office and employees from the Camarillo area would staff the office. Raymond Hanson, who had been with Joe since 1927, was chosen as Manager. Hanson selected R. Wayne Daily, who had been with the bank since the 1930s, as Assistant Cashier and Assistant Manager.

In January of 1959, Earle Glenn was named Assistant Cashier and Operations Officer responsible for working out the bookkeeping procedures for a multi-branched bank. Among his tasks were to auto-mate the bookkeeping system and to assign account numbers. Until this time, each bank patron had been dealt with by name.

Opening day, September 9, 1959, was a proud and happy one, especially for Bud Milligan and Ray Hanson. There were flowers and an impressive electronic bank vault door that opened and closed automatically. At the dedication ceremony, Bud announced the creation of an Achille Levy Memorial Scholarship, presented annually at the local high school. There was a ribbon cutting ceremony and Achille's long-time bank lawyer and old friend, Judge Charles F. Blackstock, did the honors. Bud's statement read in part:

> *"Today, with Oxnard the largest city in Ventura County with a population in excess of 35,000, the management of the bank is looking to the future, preparing for the role it must play in the Atomic Age . . . the age of space exploration, of troubled international skies.*
>
> *"It plans to meet the problems of the future as it has met those of the past . . . remaining, as always, a safe place to save and a sane place to borrow.*
>
> *"In these dynamic days," a statement from the management states, "there sometimes comes concern for the activity of the financial organization. Our staff represents a tremendous number of years collectively of service to the organization. Our ratio of capital accounts to deposits is considerably higher than the average bank in the United States today . . .*
>
> *" . . . The bank has always been a locally owned and controlled and managed institution and has every intention of remaining so. It knows that this community will grow and hopes that it will join in every aspect of that growth."* [38]

Camarillo's acceptance of Bank of A. Levy was heartening to Bud and his staff. Their efforts to provide better service to those living outside Oxnard were appreciated. In the 1960s, almost a dozen new

Opening of first office in Camarillo, 1959

offices were established.

While the communities these offices served were pleased by the added convenience of neighborhood banking, some were less than enchanted: those who set policy for the large state banks, and the old A. Levy customers who preferred to make the trek to Oxnard rather than patronize their local office. To the first group, Bank of A. Levy represented renewed banking competition and would make it necessary for them to rethink their own expansion plans.

An innovation at the Camarillo office was the drive-up window. This feature, which allowed the patron to bank without leaving his car, was appreciated for its convenience. It soon became a fixture in other offices that were built.

In addition to being the year in which the first Bank of A. Levy branch office was opened, 1959 was also the year that the bank emphatically reaffirmed its commitment to put its resources to work locally. The bank's Board of Directors agreed to play a major role in financing the Oxnard Frozen Food Cooperative which, in one stroke, assured that millions of dollars of revenue from local farms would be kept in Ventura County. Frank McGrath, a member of a prominent farm family who played a role in organizing the co-op, recalled:

> *"There was a commercial plant [for freezing pro-*
> *duce] started by some local people in Oxnard called*
> *Ventura Farms so [Bud's] group of farmers bought*
> *that and formed a co-op and Bud has been on its*
> *board of directors ever since."*[39]

The major cause for the creation of this co-op between Bank of A. Levy and the local ranchers was that prior to 1959, there were only two or three major processors of Oxnard produce. As board member Ben Nordman witnessed:

> *"Each year, Stokley's and a couple of other out of*
> *county based packers who did business in the area*
> *[forced] a tough negotiation as to what we were*
> *going to get for our products. With the leadership of*
> *18 local farmers, and Bud and the bank's support,*
> *the co-op was founded."*[40]

Since 1959, more local produce has been processed and marketed by local people. For nearly 25 years, millions of dollars a year have been recycled within the borders of Ventura County. Bud and the approximately 60 ranchers in the Oxnard Frozen Food Co-op made a considerable contribution to county prosperity and independence. Oxnard still depended on agriculture. Year-round agriculture, including tomatoes, lima beans, lettuce, lemons, avocados, strawberries, broccoli, and spinach provided the principal income for the area.

City leaders began to view the area as a major

center for the new missile and space exploration industries. The first U.S. Naval Missile and Astronautics Center was built six miles south of Oxnard. During the early 1960s, under President John F. Kennedy, the Point Mugu facility symbolized the confidence and optimism felt by American citizens about their future. It was the command center for the new Pacific Missile Range. Oxnard Air Force Base, seven miles east of the city, headquartered a flight interception squadron which played an important role in early warning activities for the Strategic Air Command.

At nearby Port Hueneme, the U.S. Naval Station included Pacific Seabees Headquarters; U.S. Naval School, Construction; U.S. Naval School, Civil Engineering Corps Officers. The Navy's Research and Development Laboratory attracted scientists from many countries and disciplines.

During these years, there was increased tension between the United States and the Soviet Union, coming to a head in the Cuban Missile Crisis of 1962. This tension resulted in an increased importance in Oxnard's contribution to the U.S. defense effort. By 1961, 10,000 civilians were employed at the bases, in addition to service personnel. The combined payroll exceeded $68 million.

In 1960 a dark cloud loomed over the horizon in the form of a water shortage. In Achille's time, most water came from artesian wells. However, sea water had begun to infiltrate these wells, causing a condition referred to as "sea water intrusion." It became clear that an additional source of water was needed.

In February of 1961, voters approved two pipeline propositions to bring Metropolitan Water District (Los Angeles aqueduct) water to Oxnard with an $8.5 million revenue bond. The introduction of Metropolitan Water District water solved the immediate threat posed by sea water intrusion, but the basic problem remains even today. In dry years, when ranchers need to pump, well levels go down and the problem worsens. In wet years, when pumping can be avoided, the natural runoff from the rains replenishes the reservoirs.

Another feature of Oxnard that changed during this decade was the eucalyptus windbreak. Since the 1880s, these fast-growing trees had been planted in long lines along roads and strategically placed rows between beet, bean and barley fields. They served to block wind movement of extremely fragile topsoil, caused by the annual plowing and dry farm cultivation of crops before irrigation was introduced in the 1940s. Now that the land was being cultivated and irrigated on a year-round basis, the winds no longer posed a threat. The trees were no longer considered necessary and many beautiful and mature eucalyptus trees were destroyed.

Oxnard kept growing and changing. From 1958 through 1963, annexation of the surrounding countryside almost doubled its land area. An estimated 40 new residents settled in the city each week as city planners and government officials encouraged new development. By 1964, the combined payrolls of the various branches of the military, fueled by the growing war in Vietnam, rose to $78 million, a leap of $20 million in just four years.

Bank of A. Levy stayed a few steps ahead of this dramatic growth. As Bud pointed out, "With the total number of depositors increasing from 9,949 in 1960 to 21,784 as of March 31, 1963, we found we had to have more room or sacrifice service, which we won't do." (Oxnard Press Courier, May 13, 1963.) The offices took care of some of the administrative load of this increased patronage, but not all of it. Bud had foreseen this eventuality. In the late 1950s, he purchased two store buildings on Fifth Street, just east of the bank's Oxnard office and administrative headquarters.

On May 13, 1963, Bud announced that work would commence July 1 on a $250,000 expansion of the Oxnard headquarters. Completion was scheduled for March 31, 1964. The expansion would provide more than 11,500 square feet of badly needed operations and administrative space. During the years from 1960 to 1963, Ventura County's population grew by 32 percent while the bank's growth was a staggering 68 percent.

Bud discussed this growth in the *Oxnard Press Courier*. He also mentioned, as evidence of its broad interests, that everything from lima beans to wild animals were to be found in the bank's ledgers: "Monkeys from Manila, both for entertainment and scientific research, elephants from Malaya and giraffes from Africa have been financed by Bank of A. Levy, as well as shipments of squid to Greece and the Philippine Islands." Concerning the status of independent banks, he concluded that through the years, a number of local independent banks had been absorbed by or merged with large chain banks. Nearly a dozen others closed for a variety of reasons. "That Bank of A. Levy has been able to survive and retain its independence is due to the persistence, pride, and recognition of its duty to repay its debt to the community that supported it and made it prosper."

The new annex was built in a modern style with an aluminum solar grid system laid over glass, and decorative ceramic tile facing. Pre-stressed concrete beams supported the new second story work area over what continues to function as a covered parking lot. Additional support for the roof was provided by steel girders which eliminated the need for interior bearing walls. It was possible to alter the interior layout without having to make structural changes. The value of foresight was to be confirmed again. Between 1964 and 1984, the bank's growth dictated countless changes to the annex.

The original floor plan featured a board room as well as a conference room that was available for community use. The president's office and general administration, as well as the trust administration, bookkeeping, and accounting operations were also housed here. An elevator to the second floor was also installed. The removal of the operational and administrative departments to the new addition permitted modification and realignment of the customer service sections providing more convenient service to customers.

A week after his speech announcing plans for the expansion of Bank of A. Levy, Bud traveled to San Francisco for the 72nd annual convention of the California Banker's Association (CBA). There he took up the president's gavel as the first banker from the Tri-County area to hold that prestigious post since the organization's founding in 1891. Only 45 years of age, Bud was introduced as the President of only one of two banks left in California to bear a person's name. The other was Bank of Alex Brown in Walnut Grove. In his speech, Bud stated he had "no startling programs to introduce," but that he hoped to set up a

Bud Milligan in his 40s

new government relations committee which would give increased emphasis to relations with the state legislature.

At a news conference following the session, he elaborated on this point. Governor Edmund G. Brown's plan for state tax withholding was opposed by the CBA, whose Board of Directors had instructed its representatives to urge defeat of the plan in the legislature. As spokesman for that group, Bud believed that benefits of the plan were questionable and the administrative costs would outweigh benefits. Banks would be forced to pay a greater amount of taxes during the first year than otherwise, and they might never become current.

Bud's organization was optimistic about the future of California's economy and did not perceive the benefits of a state withholding plan. He noted that the increasing number of people coming to the state created a growing demand for homes, goods and services: "There's no reason for them to stop coming, we haven't run out of room. Population growth is self-nourishing, because when laborers come, industry follows, which in turn attracts more people." (*Oxnard Press Courier*, May 21, 1963.) Bud believed that state revenues would increase without more bureaucratic intrusion on an individual's financial affairs. Bud's view did not prevail however, and the tax was approved.

On July 20, 1965, Bank of A. Levy celebrated its 60th anniversary of incorporation. For the occasion, Bud invited Senior Vice President Oscar T. Lawler of Security First National Bank and a friend of long standing, to deliver the keynote speech. Lawler spoke about Bud's presidency:

> "*All of us here today are aware of the bank's even greater growth during the last ten years which has . . . adhered faithfully to the same solid principles of good sense and integrity . . . Moreover, this recent progress has occurred under circumstances of increasingly intense competition and rapidly changing*

economic conditions in both the local and national scene.

"The essentials of this rare sort of accomplishment lie in the fact that (it has been done) without departure from the basic and lasting principle of integrity . . . somehow better known to and better practiced by some of our forebears than by most of us who roam these pastures in rubber tired buggies today."

On New Year's Eve of 1964, Senior Vice President T. Russell Carroll officially retired after 56 years of employment. Also a member of the Board of Directors at the time of his departure, Carroll had begun working for Achille as a bookkeeper in 1907. His rise at the bank is reminiscent of a Horatio Alger character. He was a teller in 1910; Assistant Cashier in 1922; Loan and Escrow Officer in 1929; Assistant Secretary in 1930; Vice President, Cashier, Treasurer, and member of the Board of Directors in 1950; Senior Vice President in 1958. Three generations of bank leadership had found T. Russell Carroll to be an invaluable asset because of the work ethic he embodied:

"Strict disciplinary attention to your work; know every facet of it. You have to have desire, you have to want to get ahead and not relax in your work." [41]

Carroll's hard work was not confined to business hours. His long community service record is documented in *Who's Who in the West, 1965-1966.* He became well known and widely regarded during World War II as the County Chairman of the U.S. Savings Bond drive. Carroll worked on community projects for a number of years after retirement.

In 1965, Bank of A. Levy moved north of the river for the first time and established a new office at the Ventura Marina. When his friend Walter Hoffman decided to convert the marsh lands and small private airport located off Pierpont and Seaward avenues into a marina, Bud decided to involve Bank of A. Levy in the project. Two of Ventura County's prominent pioneers agreed to wield the shovel at the ground-breaking ceremonies for Bud's new bank. Ventura's 83-year-old mayor, Charles Petit, and his brother, 82-year-old Albert, a director of the bank, were happy to be part of the project. By early summer of 1966, the two-story building was in place. A combination of dark wood and yellow stone decor, it had an abundance of natural light filtering through large glass windows.

New faces on the bank's Board of Directors reflected its commitment to the future. In 1967, four long-time directors (104 years collectively served) initiated a motion restricting the maximum age of bank directors to 70. This done, T. Russell Carroll, Joe D. Paxton, Albert Petit, and Fred C. Snodgrass voluntarily gave up their places to make room for Robert G. Dallman, Robert Martin, Ben E. Nordman, and David R. Petit. Although the latter quartet was 20 years junior to their predecessors, each had already made a name for himself in Ventura County law, business and agriculture.

In the same year, Bank of A. Levy gained television exposure on "Ralph Story's Los Angeles," a nationally televised program. Story's human interest focus devoted over 20 minutes to the bank, with an introduction saying, "If you believe that a bank must have an impressive, inspiring, indestructible sounding name [i.e. Gargantuan-Perpetual-Fidelity Trust] to be a success, then you'd never believe the success story we're about to tell you." [42] An informative short history "behind the famous pink A. Levy billboards" followed. Viewers across the nation, most of whom had never even seen an "A. Levy" billboard, wrote letters of congratulations to the bank.

At about the time Story's program was being prepared for television viewers across the land, Bud was taking on a job that would require his traveling to Hartford, Connecticut, some 10 times a year. This location was the home of Heublein, Inc., and to under-

A. A. Milligan (far right) with bank directors in lobby; from left, Dave Petit, Walter Hoffman, Bob Maulhardt, Ben Nordman, Dutch Linnett, Joe Paxton (seated), Bob Dallman (seated), Bob Martin, and Frank McGrath.

stand Bud's travels one must trek back into the 1940s and consider the fate of the not so lowly chile pepper. [43]

Bank of A. Levy found itself involved in various businesses. The Coastal Valley Canning Company in Oxnard was packing a large portion of the area's chile products (chile salsa, chili sauce, jalapeno products). Coastal Valley was doing very well. It owned the name and recipes for the Ortega products and the popular tomato juice cocktail, "Snap-E-Tom."

International firms such as Hunt's and Heinz had expressed great interest in buying the Coastal Valley Company. The owners, Jules Martin, Henry Weber and Ed Fogal had no reason to sell. Ed Fogal died in the early 1950s and Jules and Henry bought his interest. Bud and the Vujovich brothers, Frank, Tom and Jack, felt that Coastal Valley should not be allowed to fall into "foreign" hands. In 1958, Henry Weber died unexpectedly while on a vacation trip. His executor, Citizen's Bank of Los Angeles, decided to sell his half of Coastal Valley's stock. The Vujovich brothers came

129

to Bud to tell him of the Weber estate's decision, and Bud said,

> "Go ask Jules if it's okay for us [the Vujovich brothers and the A. Levy family] to buy Henry's half."

In 1960, the Vujoviches each bought one-ninth and the A. Levy group the other two-thirds of the company.

Increasing success at Coastal Valley Company, especially with the astute marketing of "Snap-E-Tom," was enjoyed by the new owners. Under the management of Jules Martin's protege, Keith McLaughlin, the company prospered. By 1966, the company's success so attracted the senior management at Heublein, Incorporated, that they made a lucrative offer to buy Coastal Valley. They also asked Bud to join their board. Bud traveled often to Hartford to represent the interests of Oxnard.

From 1965 through 1967, times were slow for the financial growth of Ventura County, and, for that matter, the nation. The explosion in the housing industry which so characterized the early 1960s had been snuffed out by high interest rates on home loans. Another reason that growth slowed down in the late '60s is because many people were financially over-extended. Bob Holt, a columnist for the *Ventura Star Free Press*, interviewed Bud on this subject on October 2, 1966, and an excerpt from the column cites his views:

> "It is a melancholy fact of financial life, Milligan feels, that the general public does not exhibit as great a sense of financial responsibility as in years gone by. For this, he believes, the banking community must bear a major share of the responsibility for making credit ever easier ... and not recognizing a need for belt tightening in the granting of loans when the margin for granting such loans was growing thin."

Bud then proceeded to comment on the immediate future of the local and national economy. Hoping the situation would improve, Bud suggested the timing would depend on the Vietnam War spending and cuts, or lack of cuts, in the social programs included in the federal budget. He added:

> *"But it isn't all the government's responsibility. Everybody's contributing to inflation. We are all spending more than we need to ... Concerning Bank of A. Levy, the financial situation has caused a somewhat more selective policy in making loans. A reduction in deposits and a greater outflow in funds nearly balanced earlier in the year, but now deposits have begun to rise again. The bank wants to be sure to have enough loan funds to take care of its own customers ... We are an independent and local bank and we have no intention of changing our status."*

Significant inflation problems started with the use of the credit card. People received them in the mail, frequently unsolicited. By early 1967, financial analysts such as Thomas Bush of the *Los Angeles Times* recognized the magnitude of the problem. "The "checkless society," a term bandied about in bank circles as the wave of the future, posed a fiscal management problem. Bush reported:

> *"The approach to the credit card held by some of our esteemed bankers has been such that not only their conservation, but also their sanity, has been questioned."* [44]

Bud Milligan had come to the same conclusion years before. In his 1959 Statement of Principle, customers of Bank of A. Levy were warned that the credit card bonanza might in fact be a financial monster. This opinion was mailed to all the bank's customers. The question of credit was pre-eminent in Bud's public statements and was a private concern as well. The prominent nature of this issue is reflected in a "Statement of Principle" sent to customers and the news media. It reveals Bud's essential philosophy:

131

"We are faced today with a multiplicity of credit plans. We do not believe they are all good . . .

" . . . Within the last generation . . . it has been made ever easier to go into debt, to spend ahead, to mortgage future income, for both durable and non-durable goods. There has been great competition among financial institutions for the privilege of making all kinds of loans . . ."[45]

Bud went on to discuss why he considered credit to potentially lead to "false prosperity." He stated that his bank was in favor of a stable economy and that loose credit stimulated inflation.

This statement exhibited the bank's concern for its patrons' welfare in the face of an overwhelmingly loose credit situation. In addition, and perhaps most importantly, it reaffirms the personal partnership aspect of banking that so many people had come to know and expect from Bank of A. Levy.

However, in 1967, with bank credit cards firmly a part of the American lifestyle, Bank of A. Levy became a charter member of the MasterCard group.

By the mid 1960s, the computer had become a necessity. Expansion of bank business created mountains of paper work. With the aid of an in-house computer system, management began computerized bookkeeping in the spring of 1965. The staff was trained in electronic data processing, and by October, the conversion was complete.

By the middle of 1969, Bud announced that the computerization of all ten offices of Bank of A. Levy was complete. It was the largest commercial installation in the county. Bud predicted a future where a person could plug a card into a telephone, making such transactions as withdrawals and eliminating the "float" by which a person would write a check and then deposit funds to cover it before it cleared. By 1973, a number of Bud's predictions had come to pass. Bank of A. Levy's computerization went outside the walls of its offices with the Oxnard Esplanade automated teller machine. In an area one-third the size of most banks, the automated teller offered most bank services with the exception of larger commercial loans. The machine made the same transactions as modern automated teller machines. The ATM's efficiency rate of 98 percent assured happy customers.

The acceptance of Bank of A. Levy's new ideas and innovations was encouraging. The bank evaluated new ideas on the basis of cost effectiveness. They were also concerned about how programs were received by the customer. In this way, Bank of A. Levy had changed little over the decades. Bud stated in 1974:

"How fast bank technology advances will depend on whether the public accepts technology as an advantage." [46]

There was a great influx of women employees into the bank during and after World War II. Most women during that era were relegated to the back rooms as bookkeepers or out front as tellers. The first woman to become a corporate officer of the bank was Marie Hudson, appointed by Joe Levy as Assistant Secretary on March 23, 1951, in recognition of her productive service since 1935. Marie distinguished herself during the Depression and war years. She was an able bank officer. When expansion took shape in 1958, Marie was the logical choice to assist Manager Ray Hanson in the new Camarillo location, a rare position for a woman during this era. Marie continued to play a key role through Hanson's and Bill Kohagen's tenures there. She retired in 1973, the bank's first highly influential female corporate officer.

The bank continued its affirmative hiring. In December of 1966, three more female employees were appointed assistant cashiers. Each was eligible to join the National Association for Bank Women (NABW). Martha Hanson was a member for the duration of her career, becoming the first Bank of A. Levy officer to be chairperson of the Santa Barbara-Ventura County organization. A large number of female officers have joined this group, three of them continuing the bank's female officers were active members of NABW. Bank of A. Levy has recognized the contributions of women, rewarding their accomplishments through promotions.

Grateful for support, Bank of A. Levy has, from the beginning, felt an obligation to contribute to the larger community. When Bud planned the bank's expansion into Camarillo and beyond, he also sought to repay the communities involved. His concern first took the form of academic scholarships for local high school students. This scholarship program evolved into a formal charitable organization, the Achille Levy Foundation. The new structure served educational, health, cultural, and charitable causes, proving to be one of Bud's greatest pleasures.

The Boy Scouts, the Girls Club, and the Fine Arts Commission in its efforts to maintain the old Carnegie Library in Oxnard, have received a sustaining amount of funds over the years. Foundation gifts have exceeded $1 million since its inception. Bud viewed these contributions as a small repayment to the selected organizations for their decades of service to the community. The formal process of seeking out those organizations most deserving of help offered personal satisfaction, as:

> "... it made us look more at those we were helping so that we would be more discerning and put our money where it would probably do more good not only in the short run but also in the long run in the community."[47]

From the start, the community has been a primary concern of Bud Milligan. His involvement in civic affairs began even before having assumed the bank presidency in 1955. Even with his added responsibilities during the next decade, Bud continued to devote much time to making his town a better place. For his many contributions, the *Oxnard Press Courier*, the town's major local newspaper, named Bud "Man of the Year" in 1966.

"It would appear that today's Bud Milligan is a rather busy man. His many functions keep him moving, and he seems to enjoy this active life. In many ways, Bud looks the part of the successful banker. His office is large and finely furnished. He wears expensive, conservative suits. He has a no-nonsense business attitude about him.

"Yet he is not pretentious about his position or his wealth. Beneath a business-like exterior, one quickly discovers a man who makes friends easily, who enjoys stimulating conversations, who will laugh at a good joke." [48]

Bud Milligan at his desk

As with Achille, Bud's family was the main focus of his hours off the job during his presidency from 1955 through 1983. Like Lucy Levy, Jeanne Milligan had a personal involvement in community activity. Sons Michael and Marshall occupied much of the Milligan's time. Bud was active on Oxnard High School's Board from 1953-1956 and found time to serve on Ojai's Thacher School Board during Marshall's enrollment at that academy.

During the 1960s, Mike had a keen interest in teaching and attended Stanford University, the alma mater of both Joe and Bud. Like many of his generation, he wanted to build the "Great Society" so eloquently described by President Johnson. In the summer of 1963, Mike joined the World University Service Project, teaching English to Chinese students in Hong Kong's roof top schools.

Upon graduation in 1966, Mike, the older of the Milligan boys, married his college sweetheart, Carole Lepper. Mike was not yet certain of their future plans. One writer noted that the newlyweds were considering their options and stated:

> *"Mike isn't bank minded, however. He and his wife are training for the Peace Corps and expect to leave soon for Kenya. Later he may go into law or the Foreign Service. Although Mike is not following Dad's footsteps, it is evident that Bud is proud of the direction his first son has taken."* [49]

Throughout 1967 and 1968, Mike and Carole worked in Kenya. The Peace Corps sent them to teach in a government-run boys school in Nanyuki, a town lying 100 miles from Nairobi, the capital of Kenya. He taught English and English literature, and she taught biology, chemistry, and health science. When they returned in 1976 to visit Kenya and West Africa, Carole reported:

> *"We saw 35 of our students. As a group, the first class did extremely well."* [50]

After the Peace Corps, they returned to Stanford, where Mike entered law school in September of 1969. While Mike studied, Carole stayed home for a year and cared for the newest Milligan, daughter Kimberley. In the autumn of 1970, Carole entered Stanford Medical School. The two diligently pursued their professional training. In 1972, Mike received his law degree and entered private practice. In 1975, Carole was awarded her medical degree. For the next four years, Mike practiced law in Palo Alto while Carole did her internship and residency in radiation therapy at Stanford Medical Center.

Although many dismissed Mike as the next Bank of A. Levy President, the person who knew him best had left the possibility open. In 1977, Bud told a reporter that:

> "For those interested in entering the banking field, a solid financial background is no longer necessary. It doesn't make any difference if college graduates majored in economics, political science, engineering, or history, as long as they study and learn to use their minds."[51]

The general relevance of the comment was appropriate to the occasion, and the timing is suggestive. Bud might have been thinking about his lawyer son in Palo Alto. Or, he may have been thinking of Mike's younger brother, Marshall.

In a newspaper article that cast doubt on Mike's future in banking, the author stated:

> "If another Levy descendent is to sit behind a desk at the bank it will probably be Bud's other son, Marshall, a 15-year-old sophomore at Thacher School in Ojai. He has shown an early interest in banking."[52]

When Marshall did go to college at Yale, he said the following:

> "I ended up taking much less economics than I expected and almost no math. I focussed on political science and as the years went along, I ended up even more into the humanities, history and English."[53]

After graduation from Yale, he chose to return west. After a year and a half of practical management experience, he enrolled in the MBA program at Stanford, graduating in 1976. He traveled in the Far East and Europe and returned to join Wells Fargo Bank's management trainee program in San Francisco. He settled in San Francisco, fully expecting a career at Wells Fargo. In 1980, he married one of his fellow Stanford MBA's and Wells Fargo Assistant Vice President, Gretchen Hartnack.

In the 1970s, Bud was optimistic about the future for both Ventura County and Bank of A. Levy. An article written in 1969 cites statistics showing continued growth in agriculture:

> "With higher prices for crops, better profit-making crops and increased farm acreage, the '70s should see agriculture continue to make strong gains, even as the overall picture of Ventura County changes. Four basic industries now account for one third of Ventura County's employment; agriculture, manufacturing, mineral production and military establishments . . . Within a fifth industry, tourism, lies some of the potential explosiveness of the '70s. Only recently has the county turned to tourism as a positive and untapped source of expansion in terms of both job opportunities and income."[54]

The diversity of Ventura County's economy would stand it well in the future, and its food raising economy would protect it from serious setbacks. This economy also affected the area's banking industry in a very healthy way.

In 1973, for the first time, Bank of A. Levy expanded outside of Ventura County. In October of that year, the Los Angeles-based Union Bank turned over its Van Nuys office at Balboa and Saticoy streets to the bank for an undisclosed sum. "Bank of A. Levy Country" had expanded its borders. Bud stated that the move into Los Angeles County by the bank "ties in with the bank's long range plan of being a consumer bank and that Ventura County and the San Fernando Valley have much in common." Bud's bank now had $95 million and 17 offices.

During the mid 1970s, there was a growing concern about the United States economy. The problem of profitability touched the Ventura Avenue Marina office; it was closed. The lesson was obvious. Expansion was not a perpetual and inevitable process. It could be a gamble. If branch expansion was no longer the best way to succeed, technology would have to take up the slack. This came with the increased use of 24-hour tellers, affectionately dubbed "A. Levy-Ators." Other innovations which made Bud's bank an industry leader were revolving credit, no-passbook savings, and an in-house trust department.

Innovations at Bank of A. Levy did not go unnoticed by the banking community. Bud's peers elected him president of the American Bankers Association (ABA) for the year from October 1977-1978. Bud's honest appraisals appealed to bankers across the country. He was optimistic, but in a guarded manner,

A. A. Milligan with first automated teller machine, the "A. Levy-Ator," 1974

recognized the necessity to "get out and hustle." Bud spurred the ABA to increase the general understanding of the banking industry's role in the free enterprise system.

Concern for the wider financial picture typified Bud's interests. During his ABA presidency, he was gone from the bank much of the time. As a result, James Koenig was appointed Chief Operations Officer. James was the liaison between the staff and Bud during his absence.

Having ensured that the business would run as usual in Oxnard, Bud went on a speaking tour. A common theme in his speeches was that profit potential should be pursued with more attention paid to reality than potential. He also discussed the prime lending rate and interest-bearing checking accounts. The most controversial subject under debate during Bud's tenure was interest-bearing checking accounts. Small banks were afraid of the added costs involved in such checking accounts. The larger institutions were less dependent on checking accounts as a source of funds.

Bud's concern for the small banker was clearly articulated and well received by his ABA peers. Such matters of immediate concern to banking were none-the-less destined to take second place to an issue which came out of the blue, the Bert Lance affair. President Jimmy Carter had named Lance as his Director of the Office of Management and Budget (OMB) in early 1977. President Carter staunchly upheld Lance's reputation as an honorable banker while a substantial conflict of interest involved Lance and his family-owned, Calhoun, Georgia-First National Bank. (*Ventura County Star Free Press*, September 12, 1977.) Lance had financed family members by allowing large overdrafts. President Carter and Lance maintained that such overdrafts were standard operating procedure among bank executives. Bud Milligan and responsible bankers across the nation disagreed. As he forcefully put it:

"I do know that this whole affair is casting a pall over the banking industry. I do know that it will give banking a black eye, if it goes unchallenged." [55]

County banker defends profession over Lance affair

ATLANTA (UPI) — Ventura County banker A. A. Milligan, president-elect of the American Bankers Association, denied today that loose banking practices attributed to Budget Director Bert Lance

News article about A. A. Milligan

On August 18, 1977, the Comptroller of the Currency, while critical of Lance, found no grounds to justify his prosecution. President Carter reiterated his faith in the Budget Director. Such presidential statements continued to stream forth in August and September of 1977.

In August of 1977, Bud was President-Elect of the prestigious American Bankers Association. By principle and reputation, he was committed to responding to the Lance affair. Later in that month, amid negative publicity concerning family banking, Bud and the national leadership of his group chose the National Credit Conference in Atlanta as their forum. Unaware that CBS Television was covering the conference, Bud spoke out in no uncertain terms against the way Bert Lance had conducted himself and President Carter's attitude that nothing was particularly wrong with the way he had acted. This part of his speech appeared on the CBS Evening News with Walter Cronkite. Jeanne Milligan was by chance watching the news that night and was quite surprised

141

to see Bud on national television.

Bud's suspicions proved correct over the next few months. Lance and his wife were proven to have indulged in huge overdrafts without sufficient notice to Georgia State Bank depositors, in violation of federal banking laws. Bud's stand on the overdraft issue was eventually proven fiscally correct.

Bud's local and national experience, and his stance on the Lance issue, had national repercussions. He became a spokesman and representative of the banking industry on national issues. People listened to his explanation of inflation's devastating effects. He decried the fact that the country did not have any leadership or organized constituency in the fight against inflation. He urged Americans to unite and respond to the menace of inflation in the same way they responded to other major events such as the bombing of Pearl Harbor. He called upon bankers to support President Carter's new, high priority fight against inflation. He believed that a balanced federal budget would be one thing that would do the most to cut the rate of inflation.

As ABA president, Bud initiated a comprehensive legislative program for fewer government regulations. His organization felt that unnecessary rules were costing bank customers and banks hundreds of millions of dollars annually. Christened "Operation Unravel," the ABA plan was specifically aimed at 44 laws, regulations, and procedures that were termed particularly costly to banking. Operation Unravel began down its long legislative road under Milligan's leadership. Eventually, under President Reagan's administration, many of its objectives were achieved.

Things in Oxnard were going well. Bud's staff, led by Chief Operations Officer James Koenig, had taken care of business during Bud's absence. While 1979 was a disastrous example of economic recession for most of the country, it was a success for Bank of

Bud Milligan with President Carter working on the Select Task Force to help fight inflation

A. Levy. In the bank's 1980 Annual Report to Shareholders, Bud noted:

> "We are finishing the second best earnings year in our history despite the economic recession which has plagued us for, in our opinion, well over a year. And we are about to complete 100 years of continuous existence in the financial community of Ventura County . . .
>
> " . . . This will doubtlessly be a trying year, but we are confident that we are ready for it no matter what conditions it produces. We shall like it better if it has few surprises, but even if it does we know we can handle them as we always have."

Bud's reference here to his competent staff served to assure the community that they were in good hands. The bank had been operating without his concentrated involvement. Bud was beginning to set the stage for his own retirement from Bank of A. Levy.

Bud Milligan in his 60s, pictured in his office at the bank's headquarters in Oxnard

Bud formally retired in January of 1983. Plans had long been underway for Mike and Marsh Milligan to assume wider responsibilities. Mike began his association with the bank in 1975, when a vacancy arose on the Board of Directors. For four years, he commuted to Oxnard for board meetings and gradually discovered that he liked banking. "I decided I was fascinated with it. It could be genetic," he explained. In April of 1979, he and Carole moved back to Ventura County. Mike's title at the time was Associate Legal Counsel and Associate Trust Officer.

He spent the next year learning about the bank's Trust Department. During this period, his brother, Marsh, also moved, leaving his position at Wells Fargo.

Both sons were involved in administrative matters, with Mike principally involved in commercial lending and computer operations. By early 1981, Mike had expanded his activities to include branch administra-

Michael S. Milligan, eldest son of Bud and Jeanne Milligan

tion and customer service while Marsh concentrated on planning and data processing. Mike reflected that this three year transition from lawyer to banker was a formidable undertaking:

> *"It's a tremendous challenge just in terms of what's out there to be met and to do, but so far, it's also been a heck of a lot of fun. It's a large amount of responsibility ... There's the whole question of 'am I here because I deserve to be or because I am a relative?' I feel a strong sense of needing to do my best simply to prove to myself that it wasn't through nepotism that I got here."* [56]

Bud approved of his sons' administrative responsibilities at the bank. "It takes younger people who have got the imagination and energy and the technical background," he explained. In 1982, the team aspect of Bank of A. Levy management was clearly underway, with Mike as President and Marsh as Executive Vice President and Chief Executive Officer.

The Board of Directors and bank officers soon felt

comfortable with the new team. Robert Maulhardt, who knew Achille and served on the Board under both Joe and Bud, wondered at first whether jealousy might be a factor. But watching Mike and Marsh relate to each other soon laid Maulhardt's fears to rest. Frank McGrath, another director, agreed:

> *"The bank is very fortunate to have those two men, alert and ambitious. It looks as though it will survive for many, many years under their leadership."*

Marshall C. Milligan

There were a number of changes to accommodate the changing financial climate in Ventura County and the San Fernando Valley. New offices were built in Saticoy and Santa Paula. The architecture of each reflected the different style of each community. Saticoy featured a modern, two-story complex with the most current technology. The new Saticoy branch was eight times the size of the old building. The Santa Paula office was located in the restored Union Bank Building at Eighth and Main streets. Fluted marble columns, native stone exterior and dark wooded interior, complete with original brass fittings and red

Marshall and Michael Milligan

Promotional coin developed for 1982 Centennial Celebration

velour hangings, reflect the Victorian era, during which Santa Paula was the most affluent town in Ventura County.

While the bank's respect for history and community is evident in Santa Paula, the modern technology in Saticoy most often occupies most of Mike's and Marsh's efforts. Fast and personal service is all important in contemporary banking. Mike recognized the trend away from the branch network and toward electronic banking, which is more efficient to operate than branches.

By late 1983, Mike and Marsh had done much to complete their commitment to electronic automation. Bank customers were now within 10 minutes drive of 24-hour banking at one of the many locations throughout Ventura County. The Trust Department uses a mini-computer to maintain and process customer accounts, and bank manuals and publications are changed and maintained with modern word processing equipment. Administrative computer terminals are used by the various offices to retrieve information electronically, resulting in ease of internal operations and better service. Personal computers enhance the internal operations and customer service of the Planning and Accounting departments. Loan administration time for financial statement analysis and projection application has gone from four hours to 20 minutes. There are more than 100 teller terminals throughout the offices, providing customers with quicker, more accurate service as well as providing bank management an analysis of each day's business activity.

In a 1984 statement to employees, Marshall Milligan described the status of Bank of A. Levy and its business philosophy:

"More competitors are selling more diverse products more aggressively to woo our customers away from us. Customer confusion is a possible result of all this competition. In our favor is the fact that we are more convenient than most of our competitors. Also,

Bank of A. Levy

OUR SECOND CENTURY

In our 2nd century of serving Ventura County, we have the financial resources and know-how that can help your business succeed. In fact, six of our seventeen offices specialize in helping you with your business banking.

...ers Office	Camarillo Office	County Center Office	Simi Office	Thousand Oaks Office	Van Nuys
...ifth St.	2245 Ventura Blvd.	5808 East Telephone Rd.	1200 Los Angeles Ave.	137 East Thousand Oaks Blvd.	16926 Sati...
...93030	Camarillo, CA 93010	Ventura, CA 93003	Simi Valley, CA 93065	Thousand Oaks, CA 91360	Van Nuys,
	987-8971	656-6035	526-1241	497-7991 or (213) 889-8643	(213) 996-7...

1982 was a very busy year for the bank, as Mike and Marsh took over as the management team and the bank celebrated its centennial.

we have the long-term relationships and proven integrity that customers hesitate to abandon. However, those advantages do not eliminate the need to match our competitors' aggressiveness.

"We are much better prepared now to be aggressively competitive than we were a year or two ago. In that time we have completed the overhaul of our operations, slimmed down to a much more efficient level of staff and . . . as a result morale is improving and momentum is building." [57]

The few hundred pioneers with whom Achille dealt during the 1880s have now grown to over 50,000 people. In the 1980s, professionals, farmers, and families are the patrons of Bank of A. Levy. Bank assets numbered in the tens of thousands during

Achille's era. They exceeded $400 million in 1984. Bank of A. Levy is in the top four percent of all banks in the United States in assets. Constant features that have endured are the quality of the human relationships involved and the natural wealth and beauty of the area.

Shortly after his retirement, Bud Milligan stated that the 100th anniversary of the bank gave him a renewed confidence in the success of the American economic system.

As Bud Milligan so aptly stated, the first century for Bank of A. Levy provided ample proof that success arises from a faithful relationship between a bank and its customers. These years were also characterized by strong, dynamic leadership, sensitive and committed to the needs of a rapidly changing community. The bank and its patrons prospered, faltered momentarily, and prospered anew, keeping pace with changes and growth throughout the country.

The bank continues to move forward, its commitment to family-oriented values and concerned leadership stronger than ever. Bank of A. Levy will continue to utilize technology and innovative thinking to guide the way into another century of prosperity and growth for the community it is proud to serve. As noted by Bud Milligan on the bank's centennial:

> *"Despite the electronic wizardry present in banks today, much of a bank's success is based on faith between the bank and its customers. We do business on faith. If you don't have faith in each other, you don't have much of a relationship."* [58]

Footnotes

1. *Thomas E. Bard Collection,* Huntington Library, San Marino, Box 15E, un-numbered, dated 1877.

2. *Bard Collection,* Box 15F, January 17, 1882 and April 5, 1882 (super-imposed over February 14, 1882). The blue stamp of "Wolff and Levy, Hueneme" blocks out the black imprint of "A. Levy and Co., Springville." See also J. H. Morrison, "Springville," Ventura County Historical Society Quarterly, (VCHSQ) (August, 1957), Volume II, No. 4 pp. 17-18. In 1878 Springville boasted two mercantile stores, a blacksmith shop, a hotel, restaurant, and two feed stores.

3. *Bank of A. Levy Files, Family History, 1853-1919,* Item 20.

4. Charles J. Daily, *This is the Life-Long History of the Daily Family.* (Santa Barbara, 1946), pp. 24-25.

5. *Hueneme Herald,* August 18, 1888. See also *Ventura Democrat* (August 13, 1885), which describes Achille's new sign.

6. Palmyre Weill, "Letter to J. A. Russell," *Bank of A. Levy Files, Family History* (June, 1957).

7. "Interview with T. Russell Carroll," conducted by Robert Pfeiler, "The Bank of A. Levy," VCHSQ, (November, 1958), pp. 10-11.

8. F. L. Fairbanks, "Early Day Banks and Banking in Ventura County," VCHSQ, (May, 1963), p. 9.

9. Loc. Cit.

10. Ibid., p. 12.

11. Louis Drapeau, *A History of 75 Years* (of the San Buenaventura Lodge No. 214), (Ventura, 1946), p. 35.

12. *Hueneme Herald* (July 19, 1894). This optimistic declaration concluded with a familiar phrase, "There is no telling what will come next."

13. Daily, C., *A Life-Long History*, p. 50.

14. Ibid., pp. 43-44.

15. "Jesse Gill Interview," *Bank of A. Levy Files*, p. 81.

16. "Lucy Sickles Thiel Interview," Ibid., p. 8. Many of these recipes are now on file at the Hueneme and Oxnard Historical Societies.

17. *Oxnard Press Courier*, Editor.

18. "Lucy Sickles Thiel Interview," Ibid., p. 10.

19. "Edward Friel interview," *Bank of A. Levy Files*, p. 12.

20. "Emerson Tucker Interview," Ibid., p. 78.

21. "Robert Grether Interview," Ibid., pp. 23-25,32; "Mike Vujovich Interview," Ibid., p. 31.

22. "Hap Maxwell Interview," Ibid., p. 38. Hap Maxwell was also a member of the Bank of America Advisory Board.

23. Loc. Cit.

24. "Dutch Linett Interview," *Bank of A. Levy Files*, p. 17.

25. A. A. Milligan quote in *Oxnard Press Courier, 'PC' Weekly Magazine*, (October 9, 1966), p. 3.

26. Loc. Cit.

27. "Emerson Tucker Interview," *Bank of A. Levy Files*. p. 30.

28. Luke Spencer quote in "System has Changed," *Thousand Oaks News Chronicle*, (June 8, 1980).

29. A. A. Milligan, "Joe Levy," *Bank of A. Levy Files*, p. 4-5.

30. Ibid., p. 5.

31. "Interview with Marshall Milligan," Ibid., p. 13.

32. "Interview with Dutch Linnett," Ibid., p. 15.

33. A. A. Milligan, "Joe Levy," Ibid., p. 5.

34. "Interview with Madeline Meidema," Ibid., p. 34. This was the 1956-57 school year.

35. "Interview with Earle Glenn," Ibid., p. 9.

36. "Interview with J. McCormick," Ibid., pp. 45-46.

37. *Oxnard Press Courier*, (January 6, 1974); *'PC' Weekly Magazine*, p. 4, reprint from an earlier statement.

38. *Camarillo Valley Sun*, (August 27, 1959), p. 1, section 2.

39. "Interview with Frank McGrath," Bank of A. Levy Files, p. 77.

40. "Interview with Ben Nordman," Ibid., p. 76.

41. T. Russell Carroll, "Fifty-Six Years a Banker with One Firm," *Ventura Star-Free Press*, (November 24, 1968), pp. 4-5.

42. Typescript from "Ralph Story's Los Angeles," *KNXT Channel 2*, Los Angeles, California. (Aired April 16 and 22, 1967).

43. Holt, "County's Top Banker," *Ventura Star Free Press*, (October 1966), p. 2.

44. Thomas W. Bush, "Is the Credit Card Pie Being Sliced Too Thin?" *Los Angeles Times*, (April 2, 1967), section F, pp. 2-4.

45. A. A. Milligan, "A Statement of Principle," *Bank of A. Levy Files*, (1966, undated).

46. *Oxnard Press Courier, 'PC' Weekly Magazine*, (January 6, 1974), p. 5.

47. "Interview with A.A. Milligan," *Bank of A. Levy Files*, p. 21.

48. Don W. Martin, "A Banker Named Bud," *Oxnard Press Courier, 'PC' Weekly Magazine*, (October 9, 1966), pp. 3-4.

49. Ibid., p. 5.

50. Jane Nolan, "Carole Milligan, 'Cancer Fighter'; A Woman of Compassion, Intelligence and Sensitivity," *Vista Magazine, Ventura Star-Free Press,* (January 23, 1983), p. 5.

51. Hal Morris, "Interview of Bud Milligan," *"The Christian Science Monitor,* (October 17, 1977), p. B-10.

52. Martin, Op. Cit., p. 5.

53. "Interview with Marshall Milligan," *Bank of A. Levy Files,* p. 15.

54. A. A. Milligan, "Area to Begin Important Decade," *American Banker,* (May 26, 1969), p. 11-A.

55. "Interview with A. A. Milligan," *Bank of A. Levy Files,* p. 16.

56. Jim Bates, "A Family Celebrates Its First Century," *Ventura Star-Free Press,* (October 21, 1982), p. A-10.

57. Marshall Milligan, "1984 Corporate Plan," *The Bank Draft,* (Bank of A. Levy Publication, September, 1983), p. 8.

58. Bates, Op. Cit., p. A-10.

References

BOOKS

Bailey, Thomas A., *The American Pageant*, (Lexington, MA, D.C. Heath and Co., 1975), pp. 734-735.

Daily, Charles J., *This is the Life-Long History of the Daily Family* (Santa Barbara, 1946), p. 34.

Daily, Wendell P., *An Album of Memories*, (Camarillo, 1946), pp. 116-117.

Drapeau, Louis, *A History of 75 Years*, (Ventura, 1946), p. 35.

Fairbanks, F. L., *Early Day Banks and Banking*, p. 9.

Galbraith, John Kenneth, *The Great Crash: 1929* (Boston, 1972), pp. 187-197.

Gutleben, Dan, *The Sugar Tramp: 1961: Oxnard Beet Sugar Factory, The Last Chapter*, (Walnut Creek, California, 1960).

Hofstadter, Richard, *The Progressive Movement, 1900-1915*, (Prentice-Hall, 1963), pp. 141-148.

Hutchison, W. H., *Oil, Land and Politics: The Career of Thomas Bard*, (University of Oklahoma, 1965), pp. 26-30.

Outland, Charles F., *Man Made Disaster: The Story of the St. Francis Dam* (Los Angeles, 1977), pp. 158-183.

Palmer, R. R., *A History of the Modern World*, (New York, 1962), p. 127.

Putnam, Ruth, *Alsace and Lorraine*, (New York, 1967), pp. 21-24.

Romasco, Albert, *The Politics of Recovery: Roosevelt's New Deal*, (Oxford, 1983), pp. 157-185.

Rothbard, Murray, *America's Great Depression,* (Kansas City, 1975), p. 122-264.

Russell, J. H., *Cattle on the Conejo,* (Santa Barbara, 1957), pp. 118-119.

Sheridan, E. M., *History of Ventura County,* (Los Angeles, 1940), 2 volumes.

Storke, Yda Anis, *A Memorial and Biographical History of Santa Barbara, San Luis Obispo and Ventura, California,* (1891), pp. 469-470.

Timoshenko, Vladimar P., "World Agriculture and the Depression," *Michigan Business Studies, Vol. 5, No. 5,* (1933), pp. 32-38.

Tuchscherer, J.M., *The Fabrics of Mulhouse and Alsace, 1801-1850,* (Leigh, England, 1972), pp. 9-12.

Vizetelly, G., *True Story of Alsace Lorraine,* (London, 1918), pp. 51-51.

PERIODICALS

American Banker, May 26, 1969, p. 11-A.

Camarillo Valley Sun, August 27, and September 3, 1959.

Conejo News, May 22, 1963, p. 3.

Houston Chronicle, October 19, 1977.

Hueneme Herald, 1888-1904.

Los Angeles Herald & Express, March 3, 1961, p. 6.

Los Angeles Times, April 2, 1967, section F, pp. 2-4 and Outlook, April 10, 1977, pp. 2-14.

Mid-Continent Banker, January 1978, pp. 37-38, 58.

Oxnard Daily Courier, 1900-1922.

Oxnard Press Courier, 1901-1974.

Simi Valley News, May 15, 1963, p. 1.

The Bank Draft, (Oxnard), September, 1983, p. 5.

The Christian Science Monitor, October 17, 1977, p. B-10.

The San Diego Union, March 18, 1978.

The West Coast Magazine, Lee Bernard McConville, "The Romance of the Lima: How the Lima Bean Growers of Ventura Valley Contended with Manipulators for a Period of Twenty Years," Volume IX, Number III, (December 1910), p. 201.

Thousand Oaks News Chronicle, 1977-1980.

Ventura County Historical Society Quarterly, 1957-1981.

Ventura Democrat, 1883-1905.

Ventura Free Press, 1890-1898.

Ventura Star-Free Press, 1966-1983.

Ventura Vidette, 1889-1891.

Western States Jewish Historical Quarterly, William M. Kramer and Norton B. Stern, "A. Levy and the Bank: From Beans to Banks in Ventura County," (January 1975), Volume III, Number 2, p. 118.

HISTORICAL COLLECTIONS

A. Levy and Bank of A. Levy History, c. 1853-1955

Bank of A. Levy Files, 1853-1919.

Thomas E. Bard Collection, Huntington Library, San Marino, California, 1870-1891.

Ventura County Red Cross Files, Irvin Cross, Director of VC Red Cross.

Index